e Brooks,

God bless you,

Stan Coffey

Heb 4:12

**Building the Greatest
Churches Since Pentecost**

Building
the
GREATEST
CHURCHES
Since
Pentecost

Stan Coffey

BROADMAN PRESS
Nashville, Tennessee

262.7
Cof

Dewey Decimal Classification: 262.7
Subject Headings: CHURCH—SERMONS
Library of Congress Catalog Number: 88-4328
Printed in the United States of America

Unless otherwise indicated, all Scripture references
are from the King James Version of the Bible.
All Scripture quotations marked (NASB) are from
the *New American Standard Bible*.
Copyright © The Lockman Foundation,
1960, 1962, 1963, 1968, 1971, 1972, 1973, 1975, 1977.
Used by permission.

328

Dedication

This book is gratefully and joyfully dedicated to my wife, Glenda, and to our children, Scott and Natalie, from whom I have drawn encouragement, strength, and help in building some of the greatest churches since Pentecost . . .

and to my mother, Adell Coffey, from whom I first heard the sweet story of Jesus and who not only taught me the Holy Scriptures, but also emphasized to me that the Bible is the infallible, inerrant Word of God.

Contents

**Building the Greatest
Churches Since Pentecost**

1

Commitment to Greatness

Serving the Lord with all humility of mind, and with many tears, and temptations which befell me by the lying in wait of the Jews:

And how I kept back nothing that was profitable unto you, but have shewed you, and have taught you publickly, and from house to house.

Testifying both to the Jews, and also to the Greeks, repentance toward God, and faith toward our Lord Jesus Christ.

Take heed therefore unto yourselves, and to all the flock, over the which the Holy Spirit hath made you overseers, to feed the church of God which he hath purchased with his own blood.

I have shewed you all things, how that so labouring ye ought to support the weak; and to remember the words of the Lord Jesus, how he said, It is more blessed to give than to receive.

Acts 20:19-21,28,35

I believe that the goal of every local, soul-winning, Bible-believing church, under the power and with the infilling of the Holy Ghost, is to build the greatest church since Pentecost.

As I look around our country today, I am excited to see that the greatest churches since the Book of Acts are being built now. The largest churches, churches that are literally shaking communities and cities for Jesus Christ, are in the largest buildings in the history of Christendom. It's the hour for evangelical Christianity that we have never known in the history of the world, and it's an encouraging sign.

You ought to be the greatest Christian you can be, the greatest churchman you can be, the greatest deacon, and the greatest soul-winner you can be—all for the glory of God. In the Bible there are certain principles of greatness we can follow and achieve this tremendous goal of building the greatest churches since Pentecost, because God's message is the same yesterday, today, and forever. What worked in the time of the apostle Paul will succeed today if we will put it into practice in our lives.

Paul surely was the greatest Christian who ever lived. He

was certainly the greatest preacher, the greatest writer, the greatest militant missionary for Christ the world has ever known. We could truly call him great. But the apostle Paul would not necessarily be great by the standards of this world. I am so grateful God does not measure greatness as the world does. The world measures greatness by beauty, brawn, brains, and bucks. That is how it is with the world, but many times he who is least in the kingdom of God will be the greatest with our Heavenly Father. The standards of God concerning greatness and the standards of this carnal world are vastly different. As we look at the apostle Paul, there are three things I think are important to remember if we would be the greatest we can be for the glory of the Lord.

The apostle Paul was great because he was committed to a great Person. In verse 19, Paul says, "Serving the Lord with all humility of mind." Paul was not a man pleaser. Paul was not in the business of catering to people and trying to please everyone. His one thought was having Jesus Christ on the throne of his heart and as the Lord of his life. Paul understood the Lordship of Jesus Christ. I believe that today our greatness, our potential is dependent upon the fact of committing ourself to the Lord Jesus Christ and allowing Him to take full control of our lives and be totally surrendered to Him.

I notice that in the average church there are so many people who have accepted Jesus as Savior, but, as I observe their lives, I fail to find the evidence that He is truly their Lord. Some have a cafeteria-style Christianity. They come down the cafeteria line, and they say to God, "I'll have some Saviorhood please, but no lordship for me, thank you." God doesn't work that way.

Jesus is called in the Bible, *the Lord Jesus Christ*. He is not only Jesus; He is not only Savior. The Bible declares that God has "highly exalted him, and given him a name which is above every name: That at the name of Jesus every knee should bow . . . And that every tongue should confess that Jesus Christ is Lord to the glory of God the Father" (Phil. 2:10-11). Jesus Christ is Lord! In the Bible, for every one time He is mentioned as Savior He is referred to as Lord eleven times. You can't have him as Savior and deny Him as Lord. You can't have fire insurance from the eternal lake of fire and refuse Jesus the right of sitting on the throne of your life and having complete dominion over you.

It is one matter to be saved but another to be surrendered. It is one thing to be consecrated, another to be converted. It's one situation when Jesus is a resident in your life but another when Jesus is president in your life. Some people claim, "Well, Brother Stan, I have accepted Jesus as my Savior, and then a few years ago, I accepted Jesus and made Him Lord of my life."

If you just made Jesus the Lord of your life a few years ago, then you just got saved a few years ago because Jesus doesn't enter in halves. He doesn't come in to be Savior and not Lord. He is the *Lord* Jesus Christ!

The Holy Spirit seemed to drain human vocabulary to teach us that Jesus Christ is Lord. He went to the kingdom of astronomy, and He said, "Jesus is the Bright and Morning Star." He went to the kingdom of botany and said, "Jesus is the Tree of Life." He went to the mineral kingdom and said, "Jesus is the Pearl of Great Price" and "the Rock of Ages." Jesus Christ is Lord. The Bible says that He is "Alpha and Omega," the "Bread of Life," "the Christ," "the Deliverer," "the Day Star," "the Everlasting God," "the Friend of

Friends," "the God of Grace," "the God of Glory." He's the Healer, the Helper, the Incarnate One, the Infinite One. He's the Just and the Justifier. He's King of kings. He's Lord of lords. He is Messiah, "the name above every name," the Omnipotent God, our peace, and our Passover. He's the Quickener of the dead, the Redeemer of the resurrection, the Savior, the truth, the Testament. He's the unspeakable gift of God and He's very God of very God. He's the way, the truth, and the life, the water of life, the express image of the invisible God, yesterday, today, and forever the same. He's Zion's hope, and He's our coming Messiah. Jesus Christ is Lord!

The apostle Paul could have been set free if he would only have offered a pinch of incense to Caesar and bowed down to his statue and declared, "Caesar is Lord," and then walked away and whispered, "I didn't really mean that, God." The apostle Paul refused to do that because he was committed to a great person, the Lord Jesus Christ.

Is Jesus Christ your Lord? I know you probably try to live a good moral life; maybe you believe you are a cut above others, but is Jesus the Lord of your life? Has He changed your life? Has He made you a new person? Is your life different since Jesus came in? Has there ever been a moment, has there ever been a time when you bowed before Him, and confessed, "Yes, Jesus, I will follow you, and you will be my Lord"? Paul was great because he was committed to a great Person.

Long ago when Toscanini led a massive orchestra in Beethoven's "Ninth Symphony," the crowd was so overwhelmed with appreciation that they gave a standing ovation to the maestro, and they cheered and applauded until finally he came to the edge of the platform. Toscanini looked at them with a stern face, and he motioned for them to sit down. Then he said, "I am nothing. You are nothing. But Beethoven is everything, is everything, is everything."

I am nothing, and you are nothing, but Jesus is everything, is everything. He's everything! Jesus is Lord. You must be committed to a great Person. But not only must you be committed to a great Person, you must be committed to a great purpose. Paul shared what was the vision of his life, the beat of his heart. He wrote, "Take heed therefore unto yourselves, and to all the flock, over which the Holy Ghost hath made you overseers, to feed the church of God, which he hath purchased with his own blood" (v. 28).

Paul, in this entire chapter, talks about his commitment to the building up, the edifying, and the strengthening of the church. I don't believe there is a higher purpose to which a Christian could commit his life than the strengthening and the building up of the local, New Testament church of which he is a part.

Today, if you want to view where God is doing His greatest work, His most abiding work, His lasting work, you'll find the Lord Jesus in the midst of the seven golden lampstands. He's in the midst of His church. Paul said "Unto him, be glory in the church, . . . Amen" (Eph. 3:21).

Many love to talk about the fallacies of the church, the mistakes of the church, and the problems of the church. I believe that every believer needs to be absolutely sold out and committed with his life's blood to serving God through his local New Testament church, and all of us need to be excited about it.

There are three responsibilities you need to remember about your church.

It is your responsibility to attend your church. I don't like to preach to people who are only here in spirit. I would much rather preach to people who are here in body, also. Spirits don't give, they don't say "Amen," and they don't come down the aisle when the invitation is given. Hebrews 10:25 affirms that we are to forsake not the assembling of ourselves together but we are to exort one another and so much the more as we see the day approaching. That means, the closer we approach the coming of our Lord, the more important it is going to be for us to be faithful in attending our church. Many people today come to church *three times*—when they are hatched, when they are matched, and when they are dispatched. They come and have a little water thrown on them; then they come and get rice thrown on them; then they come and get the dirt thrown on them, and that's it. Those are the only times they want the church. The Bible says that we are to attend our church.

We are to attend our church, but not only that, the Bible speaks of Paul's defense for the church. We are to defend our church. Paul said, "Be careful, grievous wolves are going to come in" (v. 29, author). He mentioned then the wolves from without, the wolves from within. He said, "Also of your own selves shall men arise, speaking perverse things, to draw away disciples after them" (v. 30). Oh, how we need people today who will love their church and defend it against every attack of the devil. We are living in a negative day, and that negativism has crept into the body of Christ. You would think that people are not even saved. They are negative about life and about the church. Some people remind me of a barber in a country town who depressed everyone who came in for a haircut because he was so negative. Things were always so bad and nothing was good, and if it was good, pretty soon it was going to be bad. A man entered the shop one day, and the barber asked, "What have you been doing lately?"

He replied, "Oh, I've been getting ready to take a trip."

"Oh," the barber responded, "is that right? Where are you going?"

"We are going to Rome. We are going there to see the Pope."

"Is that right?" The barber noted, "Now, Sir, let me tell you something. What airline are you going on?"

"TWA."

The barber came back with, "That's a mistake. TWA is a sorry airline. They'll lose your luggage. They'll be rude to you, and when you get to Rome, well, it stinks this time of year. You won't get to see the Pope. All the people will be gathered in Vatican Square to watch for the Pope to come out on that little shelf, and you'll just be swallowed up in the crowd. You'll never get to see him."

The man left depressed but thought he might as well go ahead with the trip. So he did and came back weeks later to get another haircut. The barber asked, "You didn't take that dumb trip, did you?"

The man said, "I sure did, and you lied to me and steered me wrong. TWA is a wonderful airline. They were courteous and served me diet drinks all the way to Rome. When I arrived they hadn't lost my baggage, and Rome is beautiful this time of the year."

The barber chimed in, "Yes, but I'll bet you didn't get to see the Pope."

The man continued, "Well, I want to talk to you about that. I was standing in Vatican Square, watching for the Pope to come out on the little shelf, and there were thousands of people around me. I thought I wasn't going to see him. Suddenly a man tapped on my shoulder and instructed, 'Sir, follow me.' So I followed him, and we entered into a big building and into an elevator. Up several flights, the doors opened, and there was the Pope. I stuck out my hand and said, 'Hello, Brother Pope.'

The barber said, "Now wait a minute. Out of all those thousands of people who were waiting to see the Pope, why in the world would he pick you out of all those thousands of people?"

The man replied, "I wondered that myself. I said, 'Brother Pope, why did you choose me out of all these thousands?' He said, 'Son, as I looked over that crowd, you undoubtedly had the worst haircut I've ever seen in all my life!"

There are too many folks like that in the church. No matter how many people are being saved, no matter how many lives are being touched, no matter how many people are being blessed, they think of something wrong You need to defend the ministry of God against those kinds of detractors and say a good word for Jesus Christ and for your church. It's your job to defend your church; it's your job to extend your church.

Paul wrote that in his ministry he taught the people publicly and from house to house, teaching them repentance toward God and faith toward the Lord Jesus Christ (see Acts 20:21). Paul was talking about extending the ministry of the church, going from house to house, telling people about Christ.

After a recent election, a political analyst gave his opinion about why an unknown man won. He found it was because the candidate had so many people going about the neighbor-hood knocking on doors, speaking to the people personally, and asking them to vote for this previously unknown man. The analyst also predicted that future battles in politics would be won on the doorsteps of America.

I believe that the future battles of Christianity, the survival of the church of Jesus Christ and His glorious saving name and power are going to be won or lost on the doorsteps of the homes of America. The Bible makes it plain that the only way to build the church is to win people to faith in Jesus Christ. That's the number one reason for the existence of any church, winning souls to His name.

Andrew Murray observed many years ago, "You are ei-ther a backslider or a soul-winner." When was the last time you had the experience of the apostle Paul who said, "[I did this] with many tears"? (v. 19). When was the last time you wept over a person lost without Jesus? God called us to go out into the highways and hedges and compel them to come in. That is what Jesus has called on every believer to do. We are to be soul-winners and if we are not soul-winners, we are backsliders.

Jesus said, "Follow me, and I will make you fishers of men" (Matt. 4:19). If you are not fishing for souls, you are not following. Nothing will substitute for soul-winning. No matter how eloquently you teach, how generously you give, how beautifully you sing, or how faithfully you serve, unless you are winning people or attempting to win them to Christ under the power of the Holy Spirit, then you are not doing what God has called you to do. God called all of us to be soul-winners. The Bible says that "He that winneth souls is wise"

(Prov. 11:30). Some cults are winning the battles on the door-steps, instead of Christian churches, because they are knocking on doors for Jesus.

One fellow in our part of the country was bothered because he was a Baptist, and these folks were coming by and knocking on his door and leaving their literature. He didn't want to talk to them and they became obnoxious. This fellow was from my part of the country. He drove a pickup truck that had a gun rack in the back; his neck was red; he was a veteran of the Marine Corps. He went to the pastor and asked, "What can I do?"

The pastor advised, "These folks don't salute the U.S. flag, and they won't sing the National Anthem, so the next time they come make them do that, and they'll go away and leave you alone."

The man said, "You mean to tell me that they don't salute the flag? They won't sing the National Anthem of the country I fought for? I'm really going to fix them!"

He went and found the biggest U.S. flag he could find and put it on the wall of his home. He found a copy of the National Anthem and taught his family all of the verses. He looked out one Saturday morning and, sure enough, a little old lady with a satchel was coming across the yard. Before she could knock on the door, he opened it, got hold of her, brought her inside, and said, "Come in here! I want you to do something before you say a word or open your mouth. We are going to do the Pledge of Allegiance." He did it, so did the lady, his children and their mamma, They all did it. Then he said, "Now, we are going to sing the National Anthem, all the verses." they sang all the verses to the National Anthem. She sang right along with them.

Proud of himself, he asked, "Now, lady, what do you think of that?"

She replied, "Well, sir, I've been an Avon lady much of my life, and I've never seen anything like this. But I'm glad you love our country, because I do, too."

We can criticize people for going door to door, but they are doing what we ought to be doing if we do what God called us to do, what the Lord Jesus Christ commissioned us to do; and that is to win souls to Jesus Christ. Evangelism is reaching out to people who are lost and en route to hell. That's commitment to a great purpose.

Paul also stressed that we must be committed to a great principle. In the forgotten Beatitude (v. 35), he said, "I've shewed you all things, how that so labouring, you ought to support the weak and to remember the words of the Lord Jesus, how he said, It is more blessed to give than to receive." That's a great principle. This world lives by the principle of receiving, but the Spirit-filled believer lives by the principle of giving. Every person is knowingly or unknowingly living by the principle of giving or the principle of receiving. Great churches are built by people under the power of the Holy Spirit who are willing to commit their lives to the principle, the life-style of giving, the giving of themselves to one another; the giving of their love; the giving of their resources; the giving of their time; the giving of their talent; the giving of all that they are. Anytime you see a great, soul-winning church where people are saved week after week, with multiple ministries, and reaching to their area and their community, bringing glory and honor to God, you can write over that church that here is a group of people who understand the principle of giving. Sometimes it is spelled W-O-R-K. It takes people who are willing to give and give and give because they understand the principle of the Lord Jesus.

Jesus said, "Give, and it shall be given unto you; good measure, pressed down, . . . running over, shall men give into your bosom" (Luke 6:38). Those who understand spiritual truths know the paradox of the Bible, and they understand that these principles work—that the way to gain is to lose, the way to live is to die, and the way to receive is to give.

The Dead Sea in the land of Palestine is a striking illustration to this fact. Located at the southern end, the Jordan River empties into the Dead Sea. As you know, no life can exist there. What a contrast it is to the beautiful Sea of Galilee at the northern part of that country where the waters of Mount Hermon feed the Sea of Galilee, and on the other side the outlet sends the water into the Jordan River. The great Sea of Galilee is filled with fish. Fishermen for centuries have taken from its waters because here is a body that receives and gives and gives and receives. That is the principle of the Word of God.

The church willing to give of itself and the Christian who is willing to give of himself and his means, his time, talents, and treasure, are going to come out ahead. They are going to in this world, but, if not, I know they are going to in the world to come because God's Word states that very clearly. The Bible says, "Honour the Lord with thy substance, and with the firstfruits of all thine increase: So shall thy barns be filled with plenty, and thy presses shall burst out with new wine" (Prov. 3:9).

There are many people today who are so protective of their schedules, pocketbooks, love, time, and of all that they have. They are afraid the church is going to get some of it. We need some people today who are willing to say, "Whatever God wants me to do, whatever God wants me to give, wherever God wants me to serve, Brother, you just call me on the phone and tell me, and I'll be there to help with the Spirit of God. You can count on me." Those are the kinds of folks we need to build a great life like that of the apostle Paul. Did anybody ever give like this man? Did anybody ever believe like this man? He said, "I bear in my body the marks of the Lord Jesus" (Gal. 6:17). Paul gave and gave and gave. He gave of his ability to write. He gave of his ability to be a missionary. He gave of his ability to be a witness. He gave of himself and when he came to the end of his road he could look back and say, "[Folks,] I have fought a good fight, I have finished my course, I have kept the faith." He looked forward to that "crown of righteousness which the Lord, the righteous judge, would shall give me at that day" (2 Tim. 4:7-8).

The principle of giving makes a great church and a great Christian!

I Met the Master

I had walked life's way with an easy tread.
Had followed where comforts and pleasures led.
Until one day in a quiet place
I met the Master face to face.

I had built my castles and reared them high
Till their towers pierced the blue of the sky.
I swore I'd rule with an iron mace
Till I met the Master face to face.

With station and rank and wealth for my goal,
Much thought for my body but none for my soul,
I had entered to win in life's mad race,
When I met the Master face to face.

I met Him and knew Him and I blushed to see
That His eyes full of sorrow were fixed on me;
And I faltered and fell at His feet that day,
While my castles melted and vanished away.

Melted and vanished and in their place
Naught else did I see but the Master's face.
And I cried aloud, "Oh make me meet
To follow the steps of Thy wounded feet."

My thought is now for the souls of men,
I have lost my life to find it again,
E'er since one day in a quiet place
I meet the Master face to face.

—Anonymous

2
Gone with the Wind

And, behold I send the promise of my Father upon you; but tarry ye in the city of Jerusalem, until ye be endued with power from on high.

And, being assembled together with them, commanded them that they should not depart from Jerusalem, but wait for the promise of the Father, which, saith he, ye have heard of me.

But ye shall receive power, after that the Holy Ghost is come upon you.

And when the day of Pentecost was fully come, they were all with one accord in one place.

And suddenly there came a sound from heaven as of a rushing mighty wind, and it filled the house where they were sitting.

And there appeared unto them cloven tongues like as of fire, and it sat upon each of them.

And they were all filled with the Holy Ghost and began to speak with other tongues as the Spirit gave them utterance.

And there were dwelling at Jerusalem Jews, devout men, out of every nation under heaven.

Now when this was noised abroad, the multitude

came together and were confounded, because that every man heard them speak in his own language.

And they were all amazed and marvelled, saying one to another, Behold, are not all these which speak Galileans? And how hear we every man in our own tongue, wherein we were born?

Luke 24:29; Acts 1:4,8; Acts 2:1-8)

Notice especially verses 2-4, "And suddenly there came a sound from heaven as of a rushing mighty wind, and it filled all the house where they were sitting. And there appeared unto them cloven tongues like as of fire and it sat upon each of them, and they were all filled with the Holy Ghost."

Several years ago Jerry Rubin wrote a book entitled *Do It*. He was talking to revolutionaries telling them that "now" was the time for action. Now was the time for revolution. He wrote, when in doubt, *burn!* Fire was and is the revolutionary god. Fire is instant theater. Fire is indeed an "incendiary" word.

Politicians seldom notice poverty except when the ghettos burn. The burning of the first draft card shook the foundations of the Pentagon. Burn the flag, burn churches, burn, burn, burn! And I'm convinced that America will either burn with the fire of a holocaust or with the fire of Pentecost! But America will burn.

Fire was one of the symbols of Pentecost found in Acts 2. When the Holy Spirit was poured out, there came a sound as of a rushing mighty wind and cloven tongues like as of fire sat upon those gathered in the upper room.

Think of those two elements: fire and wind. Fire to consume and illuminate and wind to spread the fire were the legacy of the early church. They literally set their world ablaze with the fire of the gospel of Jesus Christ. The fire of the gospel was spread by the wind of the Spirit until even an unbelieving world exclaimed of them, "These that have turned the world upside down are come hither also" (Acts 17:6).

Again and again Jesus had promised that the Holy Spirit would come. Both in Luke 24:49 and in Acts 1:4, Jesus reminded His disciples that they were to wait for "the promise of the Father." There are over nine thousand promises in the Bible, but only one is called "the promise of the Father." These words refer specifically to what Jesus said in John 14:16, "And I will pray the Father, and he shall give you another Comforter, that he may abide with you for ever."

So after Jesus had risen from the dead, after He had spent forty days with His disciples, convincing them beyond any shadow of doubt that He was alive from the dead, comforting them regarding the future, and commissioning them to go into all the world to preach the gospel, He was ready to ascend back into the presence of the Heavenly Father. By any reasonable method of psychological motivation, that was the opportune time for Jesus to say go, preach the gospel—go, start churches—go, win souls. But the record indicates that Jesus did not say to them, "go, go, go." Rather, He said, "wait, wait, wait." Don't preach the gospel, don't win souls, don't plant churches, but wait for "the promise of the Father." Wait, until you are endued with power from on high.

If the disciples who had lived in the physical presence of Jesus and who had, with their own eyes, looked upon the resurrected Christ could not perform the work of God apart from the infilling of and enduing of the Holy Spirit, then how much more should twentieth-century Christians be dependent upon that infilling of power? Jesus said, "But tarry ye in . . . Jerusalem, until ye be endued with power from on high."

If we are to build the greatest churches since Pentecost, we must appropriate the power of the Holy Spirit in everything we do. Christians and churches are defeated today because of our neglect of the Person and power of Pentecost. Many years ago Dr. E. Y. Mullins observed, "It is a strange and significant fact that Christians, for nearly two thousand years, have so generally neglected the New Testament teaching concerning the Holy Spirit." In many churches it seems that the Holy Spirit is entirely overlooked. Whether He is present or absent seems to make no real difference to anyone. Dr. John Owens aptly expressed it: "The sin of the Old Testament was the rejection of God the Father, the sin of the New Testament was rejecting God the Son, and the sin of this present age is the rejection of God the Holy Spirit."

Many believers who are genuine in their love for the Lord, His Word, and His church have never really known what it is to be filled with the power and presence of the Holy Spirit. As Dr. Adrian Rogers has said, "We've been to Calvary for pardon, but we have not been to Pentecost for power."

We need to review what happened on the day of Pentecost when there came a sound from heaven as a rushing mighty wind; for when the wind of the Spirit, the Breath of God, blew across the lives of those believers who were assembled in that upper room, their lives were mightily changed by the power of God.

Several years ago the literary world received a magnificent contribution from Margaret Mitchell. Her well-known book was *Gone with the Wind*. The book tells of life in the old South, the Civil War, and the Reconstruction period. The book points out the changes brought about by that war and about a way of life that was gone with the wind of war. This reminds me of the Book of Acts and the Day of Pentecost, when the Spirit of God blew across the fellowship of those early believers, sweeping away by the wind of the Holy Spirit those hindrances which would have prevented them from being all God wanted them to be.

As I travel, preach, and talk with and to pastors and laymen, they seem to agree that the great need of this hour is for a fresh breath of heaven to blow across our churches, our lives, and our ministries. I know that when revival comes and the Spirit of God is allowed to move among His people like that mighty rushing wind, we will be able to build the greatest churches since Pentecost because "Gone with the Wind" will be those sins that hold back revival and the power of God in our lives.

I. Gone with the Wind Was Cowardice in Witnessing

In Acts 2:4 the Scripture says, "And they were all filled with the Holy Spirit, and began to speak with other tongues as the Spirit gave them utterance." Cowardice in witnessing was gone with the wind of the Spirit, for when they were filled with the Spirit they began to speak boldly for the Lord Jesus Christ. This was in fulfillment of Acts 1:8 when Jesus prophesied, "Ye shall receive power when the Holy Ghost is come upon you: and you shall be witnesses unto me." The emphasis is not that they spoke in tongues but that they spoke the gospel of Jesus Christ in languages they had never known with such boldness that the hearers heard in their own language the marvelous message of salvation.

The Holy Spirit is sovereign. He manifests Himself as He chooses. These manifestations were definitely varied in the New Testament. But there was one thing that characterized the believers in the Book of Acts each time they experienced a fresh infilling of God's Spirit—they spoke boldly as witnesses for Jesus Christ. The one irrefutable, indispensable, indisputable evidence that one is Spirit filled is that compulsion from within to win others to Christ.

No matter what else one may claim to have in regard to spiritual gifts and manifestations, if a believer does not have a burning desire to bring the lost to salvation, one cannot claim to be Spirit filled. Allow the Spirit of God to blow fresh and new in your life, and you will be like the disciples who "cannot but speak the things which we have seen and heard" (Acts 4:20), for "gone with the wind" will be cowardice in witnessing.

This was evident in the life of Simon Peter. Before Pentecost, he denied that he was a follower of Christ, even when given a golden opportunity to take a stand for his Lord, but after the wind of God blew into that upper room Peter was willing to boldly declare to thousands of people gathered in Jerusalem: "God hath made that same Jesus, whom ye have crucified, to be both Lord and Christ" (Acts 2:36). In like manner, God can take an introverted person, who may not have native ability or formal training in public speaking or salesmanship and, through the filling of the Holy Spirit, turn that person into a dynamic and effective witness for Jesus Christ. We are told that only 5 percent of Southern Baptists ever attempt to win a person to faith in Christ. More than six thousand Southern Baptist churches did not baptize a single convert in a recent year. Why? The reason is not merely a lack of training; nor is it because they do not believe the Bible teaches that we are to be soul-winners. It is because we are not filled with the Spirit of God.

II. Gone with the Wind Will Be Coldness in Worship

Not only was cowardice in witnessing "gone with the wind," but coldness in worship was gone as well. Prior to Pentecost, the disciples were often caught up in attitudes of mediocrity and defeat. One of the disciples had betrayed the Lord, one had denied Him, and all but John had deserted Him at the cross. But when the Holy Spirit of God was poured out at Pentecost, it was joy that characterized the lives of the disciples. So unrestrained and lavish were they in their praise of their Lord that onlookers remarked, "These men are full of new wine" (Acts 2:13). Peter's sermon, which followed, was an explanation that, in effect, said, "We're drunk all right, but not on the wine of this world."

The church that would duplicate Pentecostal power must duplicate Pentecostal praise. Worship services must be characterized by joy, enthusiasm, and unrestrained love for Jesus Christ. This will be the norm when the Holy Spirit is allowed to blow His wind fresh and new upon a body of believers. Too many churches are earmarked by the opposite and, as a result, lifeless and ritualistic worship has become the enemy of evangelism and church growth. How inconsistent this is with the New Testament pattern! Even when Paul and Silas were incarcerated in a Philippian jail, they had a joy in Jesus that caused them to sing and praise God in such a manner that "the prisoners heard them" (Acts 16:25).

The Bible says in Nehemiah 8:10, "The joy of the Lord is your strength." When the joy is there, the victory is there. When the joy is there, the power is there. When the joy is there, the strength is there. There is nothing which can compare with that church whose worship services are dominated by the joy of Jesus Christ.

When word was spread that our church was a constant spirit of revival, someone from another state asked one of the pastors from our area about what was going on at San Jacinto Baptist Church in Amarillo. He replied, "That church is nothing but a pep rally for Jesus." I believe that a pep rally for Jesus is far more appropriate and effective than a funeral for Jesus. Our Lord is alive! And we need to witness like it, we need to work like it, and we need to worship like it. Jesus said we are to worship the Lord with "all your heart, and with all your soul, and with all your mind, and with all your strength" (Mark 12:30, NASB). When revival comes, gone with the wind will be coldness in worship.

Someone asked, "Brother Stan, aren't you afraid that things will get out of hand? I mean, there's so much excitement, so much enthusiasm; what if people get out of control in the services?" My reply is that I never worry about that. The problem with the average Baptist church is not that they are going to become howling fanatics by this time next week. We need to remember the words of the late and great Dr. Vance Havner who quipped, "It's easier to cool down a fanatic than it is to warm up a corpse." When Pentecost came, gone with the wind was coldness in worship, and until coldness in worship vanishes from our churches, we can never build the greatest churches since Pentecost.

III. Contention in Their Walk Was Gone with the Wind

One of the outstanding conditions preceding and following Pentecost was that believers were in "one accord." The unity of their fellowship is prominent throughout the biblical account. For example, in Acts 2:1, the Scripture says, "When the day of Pentecost was fully come, they were with one accord in one place."

Division and discord are enemies of the evangelistic church. Lack of unity is a barrier to becoming the greatest church since Pentecost. The importance of unity is seen throughout the New Testament. Paul wrote in Ephesians 4 that one of the major works of the Spirit of God is to bring us to maturity and to the unity of the faith. He instructed the Philippians that they were to strive with the same mind and heart for the sake of the gospel. The only way a church can experience this harmony and oneness of spirit is through a fresh infilling of the Spirit of God. When the Spirit of God is allowed to move mightily in a church, gone with the wind of the Spirit will be contention in the walk of the believers.

There was a time when the disciples argued about who would be greatest in the kingdom of God, and who would sit on the right hand and left hand of Jesus. But after Pentecost there is no record of jealousy on the part of others because Simon Peter was chosen of God to deliver the famous Pentecostal sermon. I have heard it well put that "There is no limit to what could be accomplished for the glory of God if no one cared who got the credit." Acts 2:47 records the glorious result of their unity, "And the Lord added to the church daily such as should be saved." A Spirit-filled church will have more people saved "by accident" than a lukewarm church will have saved "on purpose."

IV. Complacency in God's Work Was Gone with the Wind

Prior to Pentecost, these disciples had heard Jesus say, "If any man will come after me, let him deny himself, and take up his cross and follow me" (Matt. 16:24), but many times their lives were marked by complacency and not by commitment. In almost any church you can witness the same situation today. Jesus' words to the Laodiceans describe many modern believers: "Thou art neither cold nor hot," and then He said, "So then because thou art lukewarm, and neither cold nor hot, I will spue thee out of my mouth" (Rev. 3:15-16). Dr. Freddie Gage, the famous evangelist, says that many believers are "God's frozen chosen—you can't fire them up, and you can't thaw them out." Pastors everywhere lift their hands in despair and moan, "I can't motivate my people to witness—to serve—to visit—to attend faithfully." What is the answer? The answer is a heaven-sent, Holy Spirit revival, a fresh visitation from heaven resulting in repentance, restitution, and renewal.

Every believer is *indwelt* by the Spirit, but not every believer is *infilled* by the Spirit. It is one thing to be saved, quite another to be surrendered—one thing to be *converted* but another to be *consecrated;* one thing to have the Spirit *dormant* in one's life but another to have the Spirit *dominant* in one's life; one thing when the Spirit is *resident* but quite another when He is *president*.

Complacency will be replaced by commitment when an individual believer *recognizes* his spiritual plight, *relinquishes* control of his life to God, and *releases* the power of the Holy Spirit in his life.

Jesus instructed His disciples prior to His ascension, "[Wait] until ye be endued with power from on high." That is exactly what they did. They gathered in that upper room for ten days, praying and offering themselves upon the altar of obedient service to their Lord. Had we stood by that door as they entered and someone would have said, "See that group of 120 men and women. They are going to change the world. They are going to shake Caesar from his throne. They are going to defeat the very powers of death and of hell," we would have been prone to laugh. Perhaps we would have responded, "Why, that bunch? There's not a prominent person among them. They have no money, no prestige, no power, and no position." But we look back today and confess that the modern church owes its perpetuity to what happened in that upper room. What they accomplished was not in their own power, but there came a sound from heaven "as of a rushing mighty wind, and it filled all the house where they were sitting." And gone with the wind were impediments that hold back revival and spiritual fruitfulness then and now.

In view of this, my prayer is:

> Holy Spirit, breathe on me,
>   Until my heart is clean;
> Let sunshine fill its inmost part,
>   With not a cloud between.

Holy Spirit, breathe on me,
  Fill me with pow'r divine;
Kindle a flame of love and zeal
  Within this heart of mine.

Breathe on me, breathe on me,
  Holy Spirit, breathe on me;
Take thou my heart, cleanse ev'ry part,
  Holy Spirit, breathe on me.

3

A Commitment that Conquers

Now Moses kept the flock of Jethro his father in law, the priest of Midian: and he led the flock to the backside of the desert, and came to the mountain of God, even Horeb.

And the angel of the Lord appeared unto him in a flame of fire out of the midst of a bush; and he looked, and, behold, the bush burned with fire, and the bush was not consumed.

And Moses said, I will now turn aside, and see this great sight, why the bush is not burnt.

And when the Lord saw that he turned aside to see, God called unto him out of the midst of the bush, and said, Moses, Moses. And he said, Here am I.

And he said, Draw not nigh hither: put off thy shoes from off thy feet, for the place whereon thou standest is holy ground.

Moreover he said, I am the God of thy father, the God of Abraham, the God of Isaac, and the God of Jacob. And Moses hid his face; for he was afraid to look upon God.

Exodus 3:1-6

Surely one of God's mightiest was Moses. Born of Hebrew parents, he became the adopted son of Pharaoh's daughter after his own Hebrew parents had hidden him in the bulrushes of the Nile River. According to Scripture, during those early years in Egypt, "Moses was learned in all the ways of the Egyptians, and was mighty in words and in deeds" (Acts 7:22). But somewhere along the way Moses learned his true identity.

He discovered that he was not an Egyptian but a Hebrew; not a king but a slave; not the son of Pharaoh's daughter but the son of Pharaoh's servant. The Bible states that "By faith Moses, when he was come to years, refused to be called the son of Pharaoh's daughter, choosing rather to suffer affliction with the people of God, than to enjoy the pleasures of sin for a season" (Heb. 11:24-25).

Moses became great because he had a commitment to his God that conquered the devil's temptations. He conquered sinful pleasure, idle leisure, and worldly treasure. Moses turned his back on the very things which most men and women largely give their lives to possess. Moses was willing to sacrifice the worldly trappings for which people today sacrifice themselves.

Having made that all-important decision, Moses was not, yet ready to receive the greatness for which he was destined. He was a chosen vessel, yet he was not "a vessel unto honour, sanctified, and meet for the master's use, and prepared for every good work" (2 Tim. 2:21). The greatness within Moses would only be released as he was touched by the flame of God's Spirit.

So, having voluntarily cut the ties of Egypt, and having been rejected by his own people, Moses found himself on the backside of the desert with a Ph.D. degree, herding sheep! Moses, the mighty prince, had become a lowly sheep herder. I can almost hear Satan as he spoke to Moses while Moses walked across that lonely wilderness. "What a fool you are, Moses! You could be sitting on the throne of Egypt right now. You could be eating the king's meat and drinking the king's wine. You could hold in your arms a lovely Egyptian wife and enjoy all the pleasures afforded the Pharaoh himself."

But after forty years of wandering from one side of the wilderness to the other, something happened in the life of Moses that was to change the destiny of Israel and indeed alter the course of human history. God broke the forty years of silence by speaking to Moses out of a burning bush. A miraculous burning bush that was aflame but was not consumed by the fire. On that momentous day Moses stood on holy ground. He saw the fire of God, heard the voice of God, and went out to do the will of God with a commitment that conquers. From that moment on Moses walked by the sound of that voice and the light of that flame. I have heard it said that Moses spent the first forty years of his life thinking he was somebody, the next forty years of his life thinking he was nobody, and the last forty years of his life learning what God could do with a man who learned the first two lessons!

The turning point in his life was that experience of standing before the burning bush on holy ground. The greatest churches since Pentecost will be built by men and women who have shared that holy-ground experience with Moses. No life can ever be the same once one has stood on holy ground. No person can be the voice of God to speak or the arm of God to deliver until they have stood before that burning bush. Believers today need to have that burning-bush experience! We need to know the God of the burning bush. We need to experience the presence of God in our lives to the extent that we will bow before Him in reverence and humility and then go out to serve Him in the power of the Holy Spirit.

As God set that bush on fire and it burned and burned, and yet was not consumed, so God wants to set His people on fire spiritually, and He will if we will stand before Him on holy ground.

But where is the place of holy ground?

I. Holy Ground Is the Place Where the Voice of God Is Heard

It is a personal encounter between a person and God. When Moses stood before the burning bush with his attention completely arrested, his curiosity stirred to the deepest, and his mentality pitched to its highest peak, God spoke: "Put off thy shoes from off thy feet, for the place whereon thou standest is holy ground" (Ex. 3:5).

The phrase "holy ground" does not refer to the soil on the plateau on Mount Horeb. Rather the literal rendering indicates that particular piece of real estate was made holy by the presence of the true and living God. There was nothing unusual or sacred about that bush. Bible scholars believe that bush could well have been the humble acacia bush, which was not edible for even the sheep of Moses' flock; but that bush was brought to flame by the presence of the living God.

Do you remember the "holy-ground" experience in your life? Do you recall those places which in and of themselves are not sacred or special, but because it was in that special place you heard God's voice and saw God's power, they are considered "holy ground" to you?

That old country church which sat at the end of the cotton rows on my dad's farm in Western Oklahoma was certainly nothing special to see, but it will always be special in my life. There, for the very first time, I realized I was a sinner and that Jesus died on the cross and rose from the dead to be my Savior. And, in that little building, one hot August night, the altar in that country church became "holy ground" to me as I trusted Jesus Christ as my personal Savior.

Some years later when I was nineteen years of age, married, with a wife and son, God broke through in the living room in the house we called home, and again I stood before the Lord on "holy ground." I heard Him speak, not in an audible voice, but in a voice even more distinct, calling me to preach the gospel of Jesus Christ. In 1974 I attended an evangelism conference in Nashville, Tennessee, and a Howard Johnson's motel became "holy ground' as I made a life-changing commitment to adopt as my pastoral priority the building of an evangelistic church. In that moment I responded to His voice by praying, "Lord, I will pay any price necessary to reach people for Jesus."

How long has it been since you have stood on "holy ground"? It is the place where the voice of God is heard. The tragedy is that so many, even those who are pastors, deacons, and church leaders, do not realize that God wants to use all of us in a dynamic way. If we could only anticipate what God would do through us if we would stand before Him on holy ground, we would be totally amazed. God challenges us today, "Remove the shoes of worldly living; remove the shoes of carnal thinking; remove the shoes of a negative and defeated spirit, and draw near to Me in a new commitment to Christ and to the cause of building His church." Any time a believer hears the call of God to "come up higher," to make a greater and deeper commitment of their lives to His cause, they are standing on holy ground. Any time we will turn aside from the affairs of this world to stand before God's burning bush and bow to His will and listen to His voice, we stand on holy ground.

Holy ground is the place where the voice of God is heard.

II. Holy Ground Is the Place Where the Vision of God Is Revealed

As Moses observed the bush which burned and was not consumed, he began to see in that bush a deeper revelation of God's vision for his life and for his ministry. The Scripture says, "Where there is no vision, the people perish" (Prov. 30:18). The greatest vision needed is the vision of the nature and character of God Himself.

First, Moses saw in that burning bush *a vision of God's presence*. In Isaiah 63:8-9 there is a review of the history of Israel and verse 9 says, "The angel of his presence saved them." This sense of the personal and intimate reality of God came to Moses with amazing power as he stood before that flaming bush. No liberal professor could convince Moses after that experience that God is an impersonal force. No secular humanist could persuade him that God is merely a noble concept. No existential philosopher could cause Moses to believe that if God existed He was a faraway being. God said to Moses, "I AM THAT I AM" (Ex. 3:14). This phrase, "I AM," in Hebrew is closely related to God's personal name, Jehovah or Yahweh, which occurs 6,000 times in the Old Testament. It not only speaks of the timelessness of God, but the fact that He is present in every situation of life.

Second, Moses saw *a vision of God's perception*. "And the Lord said, I have surely seen the affliction of my people which are in Egypt, and have heard their cry by reason of their taskmasters; for I know their sorrows; And I am come down to deliver them out of the hand of the Egyptians and to bring them up out of that land into a good land and a large, unto the land flowing with milk and honey" (Ex. 3:7-8). God said, "I have seen"—the Hebrew word here means to gaze upon, to take heed of. He said, "I have heard"—the Hebrew word means to consider, to heed, or to perceive. He said, "I know" (v. 7)—the Hebrew word means to comprehend, to discern, or to understand. All of this indicates that God had not forgotten the needs of Moses—nor the needs of the children of Israel.

God's vision takes in the cries and the hurts of those who

are in the bondage of that cruel taskmaster, Satan himself. He has seen the oppression, the sorrow, the backbreaking bondage that sin brings. He has seen the hungry children, the broken homes, and the ruined lives. And God has sent believers into this world to be His Moses to tell the world that there is a person called Jesus who can deliver and set them free from the sin which binds and enslaves them.

Third, not only did Moses see in that bush God's presence and perception but also *God's power*. "Behold, the bush burned with fire and the bush was not consumed" (Ex. 3:2*b*). Perhaps Moses thought, *This bush has a quality I have never possessed—it does not flicker out, but it blazes on and on.* The mind of Moses may have gone back to the time when he started to be God's deliverer of his people only to see his self-efforts end in frustration and disgust. Once Moses had a dream of salvation for his people, but the dream faded and seemed impossible. But now he saw that it was not in his own self-effort, but through the power of God made available to him that he would be able to fulfill God's plan for his life. In like manner, God never can use us for His glory until we come to the end of self and to the place of total dependence on the inexhaustible power of an omnipotent God!

Our lives are like that bush. It was ordinary and common and found throughout that region, and yet God used that little bush by setting it on fire with His presence and power. In like manner, God cannot use us for greatness unless we are willing to be set on fire by the power of the Holy Spirit. All God desires is that we be available—that we be hearts and lives that He can control and burn in, so all the world might behold the power of Almighty God in us.

Holy ground brings a commitment that conquers. It is the place where the voice of God is heard, where the vision of God is revealed.

III. Holy Ground Is the Place Where the Victory of God Is Assured

In verse 10 God speaks to Moses and gives an astounding command. "Come now therefore, and I will send thee unto Pharaoh, that thou mayest bring forth my people the children of Israel out of Egypt." Hearing that he was to be the chief human agent for the liberation of thousands of people, Moses staggered before the impossibility of the task. He responded, "Who am I, that I should go unto Pharaoh?" (v. 11). Sometimes we alibi, "Lord, others are better equipped, more courageous, better educated. Why me, Lord?"

Moses questioned, yet God had given to him, on holy ground, an unforgettable illustration of how He would use him and make him victorious against every foe. God had chosen an ordinary bush, had set that bush ablaze with an unquenchable fire, and in that vivid visual lesson was instructing, "Moses, this is what I want to do with your life. I want to take a man who has failed, a man who now is nothing but an unknown, nameless shepherd, and I want to set you ablaze with a holy fire that will never go out."

Many times people have said, "Pastor, I am such a failure. How could God ever use me?" The truth is: this is the only kind of person God will ever use. Paul said, "For God hath chosen the foolish things of the world to confound the wise; and God hath chosen the weak things of the world to confound the things which are mighty" (1 Cor. 1:27). We can be like the bush that burned but was never consumed. This tells us that no mountain is too high and no ocean is to deep and no task is to difficult for the believer who has stood before the Lord on holy ground and who is aflame with the unquenchable fire of the Holy Spirit.

That bush kept on burning. The victory of God for Moses was assured. No wonder Paul said in Romans 8, "We are more than conquerers" (v. 37). No wonder he said, "Thanks be unto God, which always causeth us to triumph in Christ" (2 Cor. 2:14). We have a fire that can never be put out. We can keep on burning when sin is its blackest, the devil his meanest, and when our skies look the darkest.

When Billy Graham conducted his first New York crusade at Madison Square Garden in the early fifties, the press interviewed the famous singer Ethel Waters. A reporter asked her, "Ethel, why are you allowing yourself to be identified with this fellow Graham? Don't you know that Madison Square Garden is the graveyard of evangelists and that he is going to flop?" Ethel Waters replied, "No sir, he ain't no flop, 'cause God don't sponsor no flops."

Can we build the greatest churches since Pentecost today? The answer is a resounding yes! Through the power of Jesus Christ, made available to every believer through the indwelling and infilling of the Holy Spirit, the greatest churches since Pentecost will be built in these last days. We must once more stand before the Lord on "holy ground" where the voice of God is heard, where the vision of God is revealed, and where the victory of God is assured!

> He is today the great "I Am"
> If you are weak, He says, "I am your strength"
> If you are weary, He says, "I am your rest"
> If you are hungry, He says, "I am your bread"

If you are thirsty, He says, "I am your water"
If you are in doubt, He says, "I am your light"
If you are sorrowful, He says, "I am your joy"
If you are lonely, He says, "I am your companion"
If you are defeated, He says, "I am your victory."

4

The Message that Motivates

And when he had spoken these things, while they be-held, he was taken up; and a cloud received him out of their sight.

And while they looked stedfastly toward heaven as he went up, behold, two men stood by them in white apparel;

Which also said, Ye men of Galilee, why stand ye gazing up into heaven? this same Jesus, which is taken up from you into heaven, shall shall so come again in like manner as ye have seen him go into heaven.

Acts 1:9-11

As I talk with prophets and students of the Word of God, those who study about the signs of the second coming of the Lord, they agree that the coming of the Lord is near. Prophecy is being fulfilled on every hand. We live in the most exciting day since Jesus walked the face of the earth. Jesus is preparing to come back for His church. The signs are all about us.

In Acts 1 Jesus had been risen from the dead for forty days. The disciples were with Jesus on the Mount of Olives. Jesus had comforted His disciples about the future and had convinced them, without any shadow of doubt, that He was alive from the dead. He had commissioned them to go into all the world and preach the gospel. Immediately after the Great Commission the text says, "And when he had spoken these things, while they beheld, he was taken up; and a cloud received him out of their sight. And while they looked stedfastly toward heaven as he went up, behold, two men stood by them in white apparel; which also said, Ye men of Galilee, why stand ye gazing up into heaven? this same Jesus, which is taken up from you into heaven, shall so come in like manner as ye have seen him go into heaven" (vv. 9-11). This same Jesus is coming again.

From this passage, look at three truths. *First, there is a promise of His coming.* The Bible says, "this same Jesus, . . . shall so come." One of my most exciting thoughts is the fact that Jesus Christ is coming for me. He's coming for every one of His children. Jesus Christ is surely coming again. This is a major part of the Bible. It is not incidental—it is fundamental in the Christian faith.

Do you realize how many times Jesus promised to come again and the Bible refers to His coming again to this earth? Baptism is mentioned twenty times; repentance, seventy times; the new birth, nine times; but the second coming of Christ is mentioned 318 times in the New Testament alone. Again and again the Bible says, "Get ready because you know not what hour Jesus may come." We may look up today, and Jesus will appear in the sky and call us up to be with Him. What a thought! What a moment! What an exciting event that would be. Jesus Christ is coming again. We have the promise of His coming.

In Matthew 16:27, the Bible says, "The Son of man shall come in the glory of his Father." In Mark 8, Jesus said that He would come in the glory of the angels. In Luke 21:28, He said to lift up your heads and look up, for your "redemption draweth nigh." In John 14:2-3, Jesus said, "[Behold, I will come] I go and prepare a place for you, I will come again and receive you unto myself." In Acts 1:11 the Bible says, "This same Jesus, . . . shall so come in like manner as ye have seen him go into heaven." First Corinthians 15:25 says that He's coming to "put all enemies under his feet." And verse 52 says, He's coming "In a moment, in the twinkling of an eye." Galatians 1:4 says that He's going to "deliver us from this present, evil world." In Ephesians 5:27 the Scripture says that the Lord Jesus is coming for His bride, that He might present His church to Himself as a glorious bride; not having spots, not having wrinkles, not having blemishes, or any such thing. Philippians 3:21 says, When He comes, He's going to change these vile bodies and make them "like unto his own glorious body." Colossians 3:4 says, "When Christ, who is our life, shall appear, then shall ye also appear with him in glory." Jesus Christ is coming again. First Thessalonians 4:16 says, "The Lord himself shall descend from heaven with a shout, with the voice of the archangel, and with the trump of God: and the dead in Christ shall rise first." In Philemon, the Scripture says that Jesus is coming, and His grace will be with us until He comes. Hebrews says that unto them who look for Him, Jesus will come the second time without sin unto salvation. In 2 Peter 3:10 the Bible says that "the day of the Lord will come as a thief in the night." James 5:18 says, "Be ye also patient; stablish your hearts: for the coming of the Lord draweth night." In Jude the Scripture says that Jesus is coming with 10,000 of his saints. In Revelation the Bible pictures Jesus coming on that white horse, leading the armies of heaven, coming back to defeat the Antichrist at the battle of Armageddon and to rule and reign as King of kings and Lord of lords.

We have the promise of His coming. Jesus Christ is coming as surely as there is a sky above my head and earth beneath my feet, as surely as it takes oxygen for my lungs to have life, as surely as water quenches thirst and food allays hunger. Jesus Christ is coming again, and I believe He's coming soon. That's the promise of His coming. You read it throughout His Word. From Genesis to Revelation the Bible tells us He's coming the second time.

The Bible not only gives us the promise of His coming but also *the plan of His coming*. How is Jesus Christ coming?

Acts 1:11 says, "This same Jesus . . . shall so come in like manner as ye have seen him go into heaven." Can you imagine how these disciples felt the day they saw Jesus go back to heaven? He'd risen from the dead. They'd walked with Him for forty days. They understood that He'd died for the sins of the world, and now He was a living Savior. He was able to change lives, forgive sins, perform miracles, and now He was going to be taken from them. I can envision them as they watched Jesus. He'd given them their instructions, their marching orders. He said, "Go into the world and win souls, preach the gospel and the Holy Spirit will come upon you" (Acts 1:8, author). Then suddenly, while they beheld, as they were looking at Him, gravity for Him was suspended. He began to rise from the ground, and He rose above their heads. He went higher, above the olive trees on the Mount of Olives. He rose higher still, above even the pinnacle of the Temple— even higher until, finally, the Bible records that a cloud received Him out of their sight. As they gazed, they tried to catch a last, fleeting glimpse of Jesus as He went up into the clouds. As they looked intently, straining for that last glance of the Lord, the angels stood by and inquired, "Why do you stand gazing into heaven? You've got work to do. There's a world to win. There are souls to be saved, and, besides, this same Jesus will so come in like manner as you've seen him go" (Acts 1:11, Author).

There is no secret about how Jesus is going to come. There's no secret as to the plan of His coming. God gives it to us in His Holy Word. How is Jesus going to come back? "In like manner." Exactly as He went away. Jesus went away on a cloud. Praise God, He's coming back on a cloud! Jesus went away visibly, so He's coming back visibly. Jesus went away personally, so He's coming back personally.

Certain people try to claim that the second coming of Christ has already taken place. They contend that the second coming of Christ was when the Holy Spirit was poured out on the Day of Pentecost. They believe the second coming of Christ has already happened. It happened in a pivotal historical event such as Titus destroying the city of Jerusalem in AD 70. Don't you believe it!

The second coming of Christ is nothing less than the personal appearance of the same Jesus who died on the cross for our sins and rose again from the dead. He's coming back personally. First Thessalonians 4:16 plainly declares that the Lord Himself will descend from heaven. It will be Jesus *Himself* who comes. That's who I'm looking for, aren't you? Jesus. I'm not looking for Elijah, for Moses, for John, for Daniel. As great as they are, I'm looking for Jesus—for that Jesus who walked the dusty roads of Palestine, for that Jesus Who was transfigured on the mount of transfiguration, for that Jesus Who came out of the tomb, Who raised Lazarus from the dead, Who has nail prints in His hands from His death on the cross of Calvary for my sins. That's who I'm looking for. I'm longing to see Him.

I wasn't there. I didn't see Him with my physical eyes when He was baptized by John in the Jordan River or when He preached the great Sermon on the Mount or when He fed the five thousand with five loaves and two small fish. I didn't see Jesus when He hung upon the cross for my sins and was separated from God for me and took the agony of hell for me. My heart's cry is that of those who came to Jesus when He was preaching and said to Philip, his disciple, "Sir, we would see Jesus" (John 12:21). I'm going to see Him. That's the manner of His coming. He's coming back, visibly. He's coming back, personally, and He's coming back victoriously.

Jesus did not leave in defeat. Jesus went away in victory. He's the only man who ever could say, "I have finished the work the Father has given Me to do" (John 17:4, Author). God sent Him into this world on a mission—to defeat the power of sin, the power of the devil, and the power of hell. Jesus went to the cross and rose again from the dead, and then the Father was ready to welcome Him home and Jesus was lifted off the Mount of Olives through the power of Almighty God.

Can you imagine the victory celebration they had when He returned to heaven? I'd like to have been there. I'd like to have joined the angels as they lined old Glory Road to welcome home the conquering Christ. He went back in victory. They must have cried out shouts of hosannas as Jesus came down the golden streets of Glory, and they welcomed Him back at the great victory celebration. They must have exulted, "Lord Jesus, welcome home. Lord, you did a good job. You defeated our enemy. Lord, you're victorious, you're King of kings, you're Lord of lords." What a victory time there must have been, and when Jesus comes back, He's returning in victory.

It's going to be different from His first coming. At Christmas, we remember the birth of Jesus, His first coming. He came the first time in humility, but He'll come the second time in honor. He came the first time to a cross, the second time to a coronation. He came the first time as the Lamb of God, the second time as the Lion of the tribe of Judah. He came the first time to atone for sin, the second time to judge sinners. When He came the first time, He came to be resident, the second time president. He came the first time to the tree, the next time to the throne. He came the first time, and He stood before Pilate, but when He comes again, Pilate will stand before Him. Jesus Christ is coming in victory; that's how He's coming again. He's coming as the King of glory; He's coming as the Lord of hosts. He's coming as the Captain of the captains, the Hero of the heroes, the Master of the masters, the Mightiest of the mighty. Jesus Christ is coming. That's the plan of His coming.

I want you to consider *the purpose of His coming*. Why is Jesus Christ coming? First, He's coming for the purpose of resurrection. The Bible talks about that resurrection morning when the dead are going to be raised incorruptible. In Revelation 20:6 the Bible says, "Blessed and holy is the one who has a part in the first resurrection; over these the second death has no power" (NASB). Are you going to be a part of the first resurrection or the second resurrection? You may say, "I didn't know there were two." Well, there are two. Only the saved will be a part of the first resurrection. When a loved one dies—that grandmother, that grandad, that mom, that dad, that brother, that sister, or that friend—and you went to their funeral, your heart was broken. You heard a preacher, if it was an evangelistic church and believed the Word of God, say, "Your loved one is not in this casket. Your loved one has gone to be with the Lord. He's absent from the body, but he's present with the Lord."

When a Christian dies he goes immediately into the presence of God. They take the body and place it in the grave, but that loved one is not there. The soul, the spirit, that made them who they are, that real person who lived inside that body, is already with Jesus. You don't have to weep as those who have no hope. If you know Jesus Christ, you can rejoice at the homegoing of a loved one who's saved because they are in the very presence of Jesus Himself, and they are rejoicing in His presence. They are with the Lord the very moment they die.

They are in a place of no tears, no night, no sorrow, no death; they are with the Lord. The Bible promises that Jesus is going to raise those who are dead when He comes again. In 1 Thessalonians 4, the Bible says that even those who sleep in Jesus will God bring with Him. Multitudes are coming back with Jesus when He comes. Who would come back with Him today if we looked up and there He was? Saved believers' bodies have been placed in the grave and their spirits are with Jesus, and they're coming back with Him when He comes. They are going to come back with the Lord. Their bodies are going to be raised, and then their spirit, soul, and body will be reunited, and God will give them a new body like the body Jesus had when He rose from the dead. That body in the ground is only a shell. That body is the old, earthly tabernacle a person lived in.

A Christian man named Mr. Peas died. They buried him and put on his tombstone this epitaph. "This ain't Peas, it's just the pod. Peas shelled out and went to God." That's what happens. When Jesus comes back, they're coming back with Him, and those old pods will be raised. Wherever they're buried, wherever the elements of their bodies have gone, God will bring all of those elements back together and will transform those bodies like the body Jesus had. An incorruptible body, that's the miracle of the resurrection. Jesus is coming back so we'll have the victory even over death itself, and the physical body will be raised again. Jesus was bodily raised from the dead, and so will every believer, who has died, be bodily raised when Jesus comes back. They are coming back with Him.

He's coming back for a second reason. Not only is He coming back for resurrection, He's coming back for the rapture. The word *rapture* is an old English word that means to snatch up or catch away suddenly. The theology of the rapture is all through the Bible. The word *rapture* is not used, but it is a theological term like the word *Trinity*. You don't find the word *Trinity* anywhere in the Book, but the theology of the Trinity is taught all the way through the Book. God is one God yet in in three persons, the Father, the Son, and the Holy Spirit—and the rapture is all through this book.

What is the rapture? In 1 Thessalonians 4:16-17 the Bible tells us what the rapture is. It says, "The Lord himself shall descend from heaven with a shout, with the voice of the archangel, and with the trump of God: and the dead in Christ shall rise first. Then, we which are alive and remain shall be caught up [that's where we get that word, *rapture*] together with them . . . in the air and so shall we ever be with the Lord." That won't be the end of the world. Everyone who is unsaved will be left behind. Every mere church member who did not have the courage to come and give his life to Christ will be left behind, but every person who has been born again will hear the shout and, immediately, our bodies will be changed, and we'll rise in the air to meet our blessed Lord.

The Bible says in Philippians 3:21 that He'll change our

bodies like unto His own glorious body. First Corinthians 15:52 says, "In a moment, in the twinkling of an eye [Jesus is going to come and we're going to be caught up to meet Him in the air]." We are not even going to need Captain Kirk. Scotty won't have to beam us up. We're going to rise in the power of God when we hear the shout, the voice of the archangel, and the trump of God. We're going to begin to rise. Gravity will be suspended, and these bodies will be changed, and we'll be in the air with our Lord. What a thrilling time that's going to be!

You may counter, "That's strange that something like that will happen. Are you sure the Bible teaches that?" Not only does the Bible teach that, I want you to realize that there have already been some raptures. Some raptures have already taken place to show us what it is going to be like.

In Genesis 5 we read of a man named Enoch. The Bible says that "Enoch walked with God." Enoch was walking with God, and one day God said, "Enoch, why don't you come on to My house? We are closer to My house than we are to yours. You can come on and live with Me." The Bible says, "Enoch was translated that he should not see death" (Heb. 11:5). He did not see physical death. God simply reached down, plucked him off the face of the earth, and there he was, in the presence of God. That's how it's going to be when Jesus comes.

What happened to Elijah? He didn't die. When God finished with him here, God sent His chariot of fire, and the whirlwind of God swept down, taking Elijah into glory. He never saw physical death. He was raptured. He was taken out.

Jesus was raptured. The Bible says in Acts 1:9 "While they beheld, he was taken up." Jesus taught that when He comes, here is what is going to happen. When He comes two men will be in a field. One will be taken, the other will be left. Two will be sleeping in a bed. One will be taken, the other will be left. Two will be grinding at a mill. One will be taken, the other will be left.

We could translate that into modern terms. Two will be driving in a car. One will be taken and the other left. That car is going to go every which way if it's the driver that is taken. Two will be flying in an airplane. One will be taken and the other left. A man working for Ford Motor Company is putting fenders on cars. All of a sudden, the men down the line notice that cars are coming down the assembly line with no fenders. That man has been taken up. He's a believer. Jesus has come and raptured Him.

That's what is going to happen when Jesus comes again. That's the purpose of His coming. He's coming for every one of His children.

That's not all. The Bible teaches that He's coming for the purpose of *retribution*. God's wrath is building against the rebellion of a sinful world. Don't think that people can laugh in the face of a Holy God, that they can trample God's laws, that they can spit in God's face, that they can trample the blood of God's Son and that God will always say, "I forgive." We are now living in the time of forgiveness and of grace, but the Bible says that through the centuries of time, God has been patient and long-suffering and has been waiting for you to come and give your life to Jesus. But there is coming a time when God's wrath will finally build up and break the dam of His mercy and, like water coming over a broken dam, God's wrath will be poured out upon this earth.

In Revelation, chapters 6 through 19, the Bible describes

what will happen to you if you are left behind. Do you know what will happen to you when Jesus comes if you're not saved? Your name is on the church roll but you are not born again. You walked down an aisle but you know deep down in your heart you are not saved. You're trying to say, "I'm all-right, preacher. There was a time, way back there, when I walked down the aisle." Maybe you are living with God's tithe in your pocket; you're living with disobedience, in rebellion, in sin, in immorality. Some of you are not doing anything bad; you're just not doing anything. You're merely living a life that is ungodly, and that means a life in which you are your own god, and God is not the God of your life.

You know what will happen to you? You will be left behind, and immediately there will arise on the stage of history the most brilliant, political, and religious leader the world has ever seen. He'll have the power to do miracles; be able to call fire down from heaven. The whole world will know who he is, and the whole world will begin to worship him as God.

You say, "Well, I wouldn't worship him as God because I would know the rapture has come, and I would know that Jesus has come. I would know better, and I wouldn't be deceived." Yes you would. Second Thessalonians 2:11 says, "God shall send them strong delusion, that they should believe a lie. Now Jesus is the truth, and those who do not follow the truth will be left behind to believe the lie.

Not only that, He'll take over this world. He'll come preaching the gospel of peace, but He'll ultimately plunge the world into war. There'll be a worldwide nuclear exchange. Cities will be devastated. Maybe you saw part of the series "America" on television. That can't even begin to compare with what is going to happen. Maybe you saw "The Day

After" about the nuclear exchange between the United States and Russia. That can't even begin to compare with what the Word of God says. I wish that I could show you a movie from the Word of God. I wish I could show you the famine, the suffering, the heartache, and the hell that is going to come upon this earth. Demons are going to come out of the bottomless pit who will torment the minds and souls of people who will pray to God, begging to die but will not be able to. It will be a literal hell on earth.

There will be the mark of the beast. Without the mark of the beast, you'll not be able to buy or sell or get a job. You'll not be able to buy a carton of milk. Without the mark of the beast, you'll not be able to function in society and you'll not be able to live. Yet, if you take the mark of the beast, the Bible teaches that will mean certain hell, certain eternity in the lake of fire.

For seven years, there will be purging, judgment, famine, war, slavery, and unrest. Jesus called it the time of "great tribulation." He prophesied there will never be another time like it on the face of the earth. It will be the most awful, horrible time the earth has ever known.

You'll be separated from your loved ones. Maybe your mother is a Christian and you are not. You'll be left behind, and your mother will be taken. Maybe your brother is a Christian, but you are not. You'll be separated from that brother. You'll be separated from that Christian wife. You'll be separated from friends, relatives, and loved ones who are saved. You'll be left alone to face the Antichrist, the beast, the false prophet, and the time of tribulation.

The Bible declares it is going to be a time when people on this earth will be tormented, day and night. Following that time, you will be cast into the lake of fire, and the Bible says that the beast and the false prophet will be there, and you'll be tormented day and night forever.

You ask, "Is that literal fire?" The Bible teaches that it is literal. It's a fire like we've never known, a fire that will burn but won't consume. Most of all, you will be separated from the love of God forever and forever and forever. Can you imagine what it is going to be like to be left behind?

In India when Britain was fighting against the Indian nationals, in a certain battle, the British soldiers had sequestered themselves in a fort. They found a secret passageway that would lead them into the woods and to safety as the Indian nationals came against them. One of the British soldiers did not know they had found this passageway. They had broken up to look for it, and while the others found it, he was left behind. He came into the barracks, which were empty. He went into the mess hall. Nobody was there. He called out, "Where is everybody? Is anybody here? Where has everybody gone?" He went into room after room in that fort, and nobody was there.

He looked out, and the enemy was coming, about to break the door down. He knew he would be cruelly beaten and tortured and finally would die an excruciating death. He began to scream, "I've been left behind! I've been left behind! I've been left behind!" Frantically, he looked for the way out where his fellow soldiers must have gone. He found it! The soldiers reported that the young man's hair which had been jet black had turned completely white because of the fear that the men had gone and left him behind.

That's why the Bible says that when Jesus comes, every unsaved person will mourn because of Him. They'll cry for the rocks and the mountains to fall on them and yell, "Hide us from the wrath of the Lamb," but there'll be no place to hide.

If Jesus came today, do you know that you'd be taken up to be with Him? If Jesus came today, are you sure, beyond any doubt, that you are a child of God? If you say, "I'm not quite sure. I can't remember what I did back there when I made that decision. I just can't remember what happened, I'm just not sure that I did what the Bible says to be saved. What do I need to do?" you need to draw a line on the past.

You need to say, "I don't know what I did back there, but I know today that Jesus is coming and that I want to be saved and want to be ready to meet Him." You can say, "Lord Jesus, regardless of what I did in the past, I want to call on you now to save me. I want to be ready when You come. Oh God, save me!" and God will save you today!

5

Condition of the Lost

Wherefore remember, that ye being in time past Gentiles in the flesh, who are called Uncircumcision by that which is called the circumcision in the flesh made by hands.

That at that time ye were without Christ, being aliens from the commonwealth of Israel, and strangers from the convenants of promise, having no hope, and without God in the world.

But now in Christ Jesus ye who sometimes were far off are made nigh by the blood of Christ.

For he is our peace, who hath made both one, and hath broken down the middle wall of partition between us.

Ephesians 2:11-14

Notice how the apostle Paul describes the condition of lost men. He is reminding the Ephesians of what it is to be lost. It is possible to be saved and be a part of the things of God, to be so used to and accustomed to the Lord's people, the Lord's house, and the Lord's ways that we forget what it was to be lost.

I can look into the faces of people who, only a few months or years ago, did not know the Lord Jesus Christ. Only a short time ago they were on their way to a devil's hell. The apostle Paul reminds all of us what it was like before Jesus came into our lives and saved us.

Notice verse 12 in the second chapter of Ephesians as we look at what it means to be lost.

Very few times in the Bible does God use the word *lost* to describe the unsaved condition of people without Jesus. In Luke 19:10 Jesus said that "the Son of man is come to seek and to save that which was lost." Three times in Luke 15, Jesus described a man without Christ as being lost. He talked about the lost sheep and the lost coin and the lost son, and then He told about how the lost was found and brought to God.

What do you think of when you hear the word, *lost?* What does *L-O-S-T* mean to you? What does it really mean when a person is lost without the Lord Jesus Christ?

We need to understand what it is to be lost because we'll never pray as we ought to pray, never witness as we ought to witness, and never have the burden God wants us to have until we see what it is to be lost without Jesus Christ.

William Booth, the powerful soul-winner and founder of the Salvation Army, was once asked, "Do you think you have the best witnessing school in the world? Do you think you have the best training program to teach people how to witness for Jesus Christ and win souls to Jesus?" He had trained literally thousands of people to witness on the street to those who were less fortunate and win them to faith in Christ.

William Booth replied, "No, I don't think my methods are the best methods. I think the best method of giving people a burden for lost souls would be to take them to the devil's hell and allow them to experience what it is to be lost in hell, separated from God for an eternity in the fire that could never be quenched. Then, I believe, men would truly have a burden and know what it is to be soul-winners because they would see what it is to be lost."

Ephesians 2:12 is one of the best descriptions in the Bible about what it is to be lost. It says, "That at that time ye were without Christ, being aliens from the commonwealth of Israel, and strangers from the covenants of promise, having no hope, and without God in the world."

Notice that to be lost is to be Christless. At that time, you were without Christ. The Gentile world, you see, had no

Messiah. They had no Deliverer who would come. They had no hope in Jesus Christ. They had no Savior. Is there any poverty more destitute than the poverty to be without a Lord on which to call and a Savior to whom you could pray and a God that would help you? All that Jesus came to do, the lost had no part in. All that Jesus means to us, the birth of Christ at Christmas, the resurrection of Jesus at Easter has no meaning for those who are lost, because the Bible says they are without Christ.

In 1 Corinthians 13, that great love chapter, Paul speaks about the power of love and what it means to be without love. If you read this chapter and substitute the word *Christ* for the word *charity* or *love,* you would get an idea of what it means to be lost. No matter what else a person has, if he doesn't have Christ, he is poor indeed.

Paul could have said, "Though I speak with the tongues of men and of angels, and have not Christ, I am become as sounding brass, or a tinkling cymbal. And though I have the gift of prophecy, and understand all mysteries, and all knowledge; . . . and have not Christ, I am nothing. And though I bestow all my goods to feed the poor, and though I give my body to be burned, and have not Christ, it profiteth me nothing." To be lost means to be Christless.

Then Paul says that to be lost means to be churchless. Notice he says that not only is it to be without Christ but it is to be an alien from the commonwealth of Israel.

In a sense, the church can be compared to what Israel was in the Old Testament. The church and Israel are distinctly separate in the Word of God. Yet, we see a comparison, because both are, in a very real sense, the family of God in a special way. So Paul is stating in this particular passage *that to be lost means to be an alien from the family of God.* To be an alien means not to be at home as opposed to feeling completely at home. The lost person doesn't feel at home in the family of God.

We sing, "I'm so glad I'm a part of the family of God; I've been washed in the fountain, cleansed by His blood," and oh, what it means to us to come into this place and be a part of God's family! But all of that means nothing to someone who is lost. He is churchless. He is not a part of the called-out disciples of the Lord. We sing the hymns of the faith, and they bless our hearts. He hears the hymns of the faith, and they mean nothing to him. We love to hear the preaching of the Word of God and the sweet Scripture that God gives us in His Word, but it means nothing to him. He has no point of reference because he is churchless. "He is alienated, a stranger," the Bible teaches. He is not at home in the family of God.

It also says he is an alien from the *commonwealth* of Israel. The word "commonwealth" in verse 12 has to do with the rights of citizenship. The person who is not a child of God is not a citizen of the kingdom of God. He has no citizenship rights. He has no citizenship privileges. He has not citizenship responsibilities. So to be lost, first of all, means to be Christless, and then it means to be churchless.

Notice, third, it means promiselessness. He says that they are "strangers from the covenants of promise." All the promises of God we have in His Word mean nothing to him. The promise of God to answer prayer means nothing to him. The promise of God to meet the needs of His children means nothing to him. He is without a promise. All the thousands of promises of God that we cling to, that we hold to, mean nothing to the people who don't know Jesus, because they're lost.

They are aliens from the commonwealth of Israel, "strangers from the convenants of promise," particularly the promise of life in Jesus Christ. Every promise of peace, security, joy, and blessing means nothing to one who is lost and has no part in the promises of God.

Now notice, number four, that not only does it mean to be without promise but *it means to be hopeless*. Paul also says in verse 12, ". . . having no hope." Don't read that lightly. The person without Jesus has no hope.

What does it mean to be lost? It means that 60,000 people in Amarillo are churchless, and many of them are lost, without Jesus Christ. What does it mean when you have to think about the thousands of people in your city who don't know the Lord? It means they are without hope.

In Dante's *Divine Comedy,* he pictures hell as a giant door leading into the bottomless pit and over that door is written the words, "All hope abandon, ye who enter here." He has no hope. He has not one shred of hope, not a ray of light of hope, not one second of hope. No matter what else he may have in his life, the person without Jesus is absolutely devoid of hope. When he goes to the graveyard and the funeral and he buries his loved ones, when the clods fall on the casket, they are saying to him, "No hope, no hope, no hope."

That neighbor you know without Jesus, that man where you work who is lost without Christ, that teenager who sits across from you in a classroom, that friend you know who has never given his life to Jesus Christ is without hope. He may have a good job, but he has no hope. He may have a family, but he has no hope. He may have a beautiful home, but he has no hope. He may have plenty of money, but he has no hope. The Bible says that he is without hope in this world. Can you image what that is like? Do you know what it means when you have no hope?

Have you ever sat in a hospital waiting room when a member of your family was having exploratory surgery, and the doctor comes out, shakes his head, looks into your face, and says about your loved one, "I'm sorry, there's no hope. There's nothing I can do"? Do you know what it is, after many days of your loved one's sickness in a hospital, to enter the room of that loved one and have the doctor come in for the last time, turn to you, and report, "There's no hope"?

One of the saddest things in the Bible is this word in Ephesians 2:12, that a lost man has no hope. No hope of salvation, no hope of forgiveness, no hope of life, no hope of joy, no hope of seeing Jesus, no hope of seeing his loved ones again. He is absolutely without hope. It means to be hopeless.

Now notice, fifth, to be lost means to be godless. Paul goes on to say. ". . . having no hope, and without God in the world." Do you know what it means to be godless? To be godless means, in one sense, to be immoral but to be godless means more than that. I know many people who are godless people. They live godless lives, and yet they are very moral people. I know people who are honest, who pay their debts. I know people who are "good ole Joes." I know people who are involved in community activities and are godless people. To be godless doesn't necessarily mean to be immoral. To be godless means to live your life apart from God. It means to live your life without calling on God for salvation, without trusting in God for His help, without knowing God's Son. To live your life apart from God is to be godless.

I've known people who are members of the church, whose names are on the church rolls, but I have to say that they are godless people. They come to church on Sunday morning, but they live most of their lives without any thought of God, without any commitment to God. To be lost means to be godless.

If you are living your life apart from the will of God for your life, apart from God's direction in your life, apart from dependence upon God in your life, you are living a godless kind of life. Does this describe anybody you know?

The Bible makes it plain that they are without Christ, without hope, and they are without God in this world. They can't look to God for His will or His direction. They are lost.

What does it mean to be lost? The word *lost* is terrible. It's terrible when someone has to admit, "I've lost my health." The health and strength and youth they once knew is gone and disease has come and their body is weakened. It is terrible to lose your health. We ought to thank God every day for our health, that we can work, that we have the strength to go out and earn a living. What a blessing it is. What about when someone has to say, "I've lost my health," and it can never be regained?

It's terrible for someone to moan, "I've lost my family." I've known men who thought that they were in love with somebody else. I've known women who thought they were in love with somebody else. They were infatuated. They became involved with somebody else, and then when it was too late, they had lost their family, and they would come and plead, "Preacher, I've lost my family. Help me get them back." I know there are people tonight who would give anything they have in this world only to have back that family they found out means so much to them. But they've lost their family, and it will never be the same again. It's lost.

I've known men who've lost their fortunes, men who've lost their businesses, men who've invested their life savings in a particular project and overnight lost everything they had. What a terrible word is *lost* when someone comes and cries, "Oh, I have lost everything I own."

I read about a family in Amarillo who had a fire in their home. It was said they lost everything they had. What a horrible tragedy for a fire to come in the cold of the winter and people to be outside of their home watching everything they have going up in smoke; but there is no sadness in this world to compare with a person who has to confess, "I have lost my soul." That's the greatest loss of all.

Paul writes that we don't have to be lost. In verse 13, he says, "But now in Christ Jesus ye who sometimes were far off are made nigh by the blood of Christ."

Harry Pastorious was a lost man. He was Christless. He didn't know Christ. He was churchless. He had never been a part of the family of God. He was promiseless. He didn't know anything about the promise of eternal life or the promises of God to the believer. He had absolutely no hope. He was godless. He had lived his life without God, but a deacon in the First Baptist Church of Albuquerque was faithful in witnessing to this man and sharing Jesus Christ with him. He was one of those people hard to win. He was an engineer, an intelligent man. He was morally upright. Sometimes, those are the worst kind, the hardest kind to win, because they don't see any need for God. He had everything he needed. He had a good job, a good retirement, a beautiful home, and everything he thought he would ever need. He didn't need God.

One day he found that he had cancer, and it was serious. The deacon began to witness to him even more because he knew that as cancer began to take his body, little by little, and snuff out his life, that man would need salvation and Jesus Christ as never before. He thought, *Maybe now he'll listen.* At first, he still wouldn't listen. Pretty soon, he confided, "I need to know more about this Jesus."

One day, Bob called me and said, "Brother Stan, I want you to go out and see a friend of mine. I've been witnessing to him for several years. He's a hard and proud man, but he's dying of cancer, and he knows it. He said that it would be all right if you came to see him."

I went and shared the story with him that he had heard many times from Bob. Bob had planted the seed, and I just went out, watered the seed a little, shared Jesus with him, went back a second time, and he gave his life to Christ. This man, who was churchless, Christless, godless, and who didn't need God, had a joy that he didn't think possible. He had never before understood. Finally, the light dawned in his soul, and his whole life changed. His wife testified that she couldn't believe the miracle she saw in his life. He still had the cancer, but his whole attitude, his whole outlook, had changed.

We wanted to see him baptized and hoped that he could come to the church for baptism, but the doctor wouldn't allow him to do it. One night, we simply decided that we'd have baptism and communion. He said, "Preacher, I've wasted my life, but one thing I've always wanted to do, if it was real, was have communion. I've never gotten to participate in that because I've never been a Christian. I want to have communion, and I want my friends to be here. I've got a lot of friends who don't know Jesus, and they're lost, just like I was. They can't believe the change that they see in me. Every time they come to see me, they are amazed because of my attitude. They see a difference in my life, and they can't believe it. Preacher, we are going to invite all of those people to my house. You're going to baptize me in the bathtub, and we're going to have a communion service, and I'm going to give my testimony to my friends."

We had one of the greatest services I've ever seen in my life. We didn't ask anybody at all. We didn't have any better sense than to fill the tub up with water. He got down in that tub, as that deacon looked on, and I baptized that man in the name of the Father and the Son and the Holy Spirit. The house was filled with people, many of whom did not know Jesus as their Savior, and they witnessed this man and his testimony for Christ. Then we had the Lord's Supper and, for the first time, he knew what it was to be a Christian and to have Christ. Gathered around him were the people who had prayed for him and loved him through the years, and he knew what it was to have a family of God. No longer was he an alien from the commonwealth of Israel. No longer was he a stranger from the covenant of promise. Now, he had been made "nigh by the blood of Jesus Christ." I saw that man die. That man died like a Christian with his faith and his trust in the Lord Jesus Christ.

All over our city and all over our world there are men like that who are lost, who are Christless, who are churchless, who are without God, who are hopeless, who have absolutely no hope, and if you'll be faithful in sharing the gospel and faithful in your witness to them, if you'll be faithful in praying for them, if you'll be faithful in planting the seed for them, God is going to give you the opportunity to see them come to know Christ as Savior and Lord.

I challenged my staff to seek to win at least one soul to Christ every week, our deacons and teachers to seek to win at least one soul every month. Only with God's help, only in the power of the Holy Spirit can this be done. I've asked all of my people to seek and win at least one lost sheep to Jesus in the coming year. I believe, under God, if ever there was a church in this world that could do it, ours is the church that God can use. We've seen more than three thousand people come to know Christ. We have a plan for winning Amarillo to Jesus, and this is the plan. The plan is to one on one, heart to heart, eye to eye, share Jesus Christ in our daily traffic pattern of life and to equip as many as we can to be flaming witnesses for Jesus Christ.

This plan is about reaching people who are lost, without hope, without God, without Christ, and bringing them into the fold of God. It's about going after that lost sheep and bringing him in.

What a responsibility we have unto God to do it now.

6

Appointed and Anointed for Greatness

And he came to Nazareth, where he had been brought up: and as the custom was, he went into the synagogue on the sabbath day, and stood up for to read.

And there was delivered to him the book of the prophet Esaias. And when he had opened the book he found the place where it was written,

The Spirit of the Lord is upon me, because he hath anointed me to preach the gospel to the poor; he hath sent me to heal the brokenhearted, to preach deliverance to the captives, and recovering of sight to the blind, to set at liberty them that are bruised,

To preach the acceptable year of the Lord.

Luke 4:16-19

I thank God that when He called me to preach, I was appointed and I was anointed for service.

I was reared in a little town in Oklahoma called Sweetwater, which is about fifteen miles northwest of Sayre. I can never remember a time when I did not attend church and Sunday School. I grew up in a Christian home. My dad was a cotton farmer, and I attended a little Southern Baptist church that was located at the end of the cotton rows on my dad's farm. It wasn't one of these big, fancy churches but one that had about three rooms and a path. I was "ordained" every year to help clean away that path.

About the third week of every August we had a revival meeting and if anyone in the community wanted to be saved, wanted to be blessed, wanted to be baptized, or wanted anything spiritually to happen they had to wait until the third week of August, because that was the time God always met with us. Those preachers would come out there, and they would preach! I never heard anything, when I was a boy, about the JEPD theory of the Pentateuch or the Book of Second Isaiah. Those preachers came out there, and they preached that sin was black, hell hot, heaven sweet, judgment sure, and Jesus saves!

One night while a country preacher was preaching about the love of God, I heard him declare that when God loved, He loved the world, and when God gave, He gave His Son, and that Jesus Christ had come to save me. I realized I was a sinner and that my mother, dad, and sister had something I didn't have, and that was salvation in Jesus Christ.

I heard him ask, "What will you do with Jesus who is called Christ?" And I answered in my heart, "I am going to repent of my sin and trust Him as my Lord and Savior," and Jesus came to live in my life, and He has been there ever since, and He is there right now. My heart was so full of joy and excitement about winning my friends to Christ. I would bring my little friends from school to church and to revival meetings and when they'd get saved, my heart would be filled with joy.

When I was about nine years of age, I held my first prayer meeting service. God hadn't called me to preach yet. Then, when I was sixteen, I was Church Training director. All through those years He was trying, I believe, to break through into my heart to show me what He had for me to do, but I didn't hear His voice until I was nineteen years of age. I was in college and married, and when God called me to preach, He called my wife also. When I told her, I thought it would be big news, but she only said, "Honey, what's taken you so long? I've known God was calling you into the ministry all of this time." So we quit our jobs and moved to one of our fine Baptist schools, Wayland Baptist College in Plainview, Texas, and the Lord blessed there. In about three months, God gave me my first church. That was in April of 1967, and God has been so good. I have not been without a church since that time. I have been continuously pastoring through college and seminary.

In my last year of seminary I moved to a place called Texarkana, Arkansas, and the Trinity Baptist Church, four miles out in the country. We were running about two hundred in Sunday School, and there was a strange hunger in my heart. I looked about at my contemporaries, at the men God used, and I looked at my own ministry, and I prayed, "God, I wish you could use me like you are using some of these men that I love so much. God, I wish you could do something in my life." My wife even sensed it and said, "You know, Stan, I think God wants to do so much more in you than you are allowing Him to do."

I went to a conference in Nashville, Tennessee, at the Park Avenue Baptist Church. My associate pastor, Dennis Sewell, went with me. As we were in that conference, I heard a preacher preach on the subject, "Without a Vision, the People Perish," and he talked about the fact that God gives people a vision and then supplies the spiritual vitality—and that anyone can be used of God if he'll make himself available to the Holy Spirit. There wasn't any loud thunder, no lightning flashed, and no earthquake happened; but on my knees in the motel room at Nashville, I came to a new understanding of what it meant to be available to God.

I prayed, "God, whatever it takes, I want to be used of you. Whatever you have to do in my life, whatever you have to do in the lives of my family, my wife, my home, God, I want to be what You want me to be." My life has been different since that time. Before then, the most I had ever baptized in one year was about seventy people. That very year, I baptized 210 people and was second in the state of Arkansas in baptisms. The next year, I baptized 243. The next year, I baptized 283. The next year, I baptized 661. The next year, I baptized more than 1,100. God sent me to Albuquerque, New Mexico, where people were predominantly Catholics and in only two years time we baptized more than 1,100 people as God was moving and working mightily. Our ratio of baptisms last year was eight to one. In the SBC it is about forty-five to one. I'm not bragging on Stan Coffey today. I'm just saying that something happened in my life that made my ministry different.

Let me tell you what happened. There were three truths that God showed me when my life and ministry turned the corner.

First of all, God showed me that I was appointed in the plan of God. I realized that when God called me He didn't need another W. A. Criswell. When God called me He didn't need another Billy Graham. When God called me He didn't need another Bailey Smith. When God called me He needed a Stan Coffey, and that is why He called me since I was uniquely equipped to be Stan Coffey. Nobody could be successful at being Stan Coffey and doing what God wanted Stan Coffey to do but Stan Coffey. I'm a designer's original—nobody else like me. Our deacons say, "Thank God."

Preachers have a problem with trying to model their ministry after somebody else. Every young preacher does that. In the last century there were so many preachers who tried to model themselves after Dr. Broaddus. Dr. Broaddus had studied so long that his shoulders were stooped and almost anywhere you would go in the entire Southern Baptist Convention, to a meeting or an evangelism conference, the preacher would be up there in the pulpit with a stooped shoulder. They all wanted to be like Dr. Broaddus.

Then there was Billy Sunday, so dynamic and so mightily used of God. A preacher in Missouri said, "I've got to find the secret of being used of God and having all those people saved. I'm going to find out from Billy Sunday." He went to a Billy Sunday meeting and there was the "sawdust trail," the tent, and the crowds. He watched Billy Sunday mount the platform and very boldly look out over the crowd and say, "Now I'm gonna get mighty hard on you he devils and all you she devils here tonight!" Then he watched Billy Sunday as he went through all of his antics. Billy Sunday said, "As long as I've got a fist, I'm gonna clobber the devil, and as long as I've got a foot, I'm gonna kick the devil, and as long as I've got teeth, I'm gonna bite the devil, and when I lose my teeth, I'm gonna gum him to death!"

The preacher thought, *That's the secret, I'm a coward.* He went back out to his country church with forty people. Sunday morning came. Forty people there. He stood behind the pulpit, and he hollered, "I'm gonna be mighty hard on all you he devils and all you she devils here this morning." Man, he began to preach like he had seen Billy Sunday do. He took the chair, hit the devil over the head with it, and broke the chair, and the whole congregation fled in terror out the back door, but they came back that night at six o'clock and fired him!

Then, of course, everybody wanted to be like Dr. R. G. Lee. One fellow wanted to be like him so badly. He studied Dr. Lee's sermons until he got all those adjectives just right, all in a string, like a string of pearls, and still he complained, "I've failed, I'm not Dr. Lee. Dr. Lee dresses in white suits."

So he bought a white suit, and every Sunday he wore the white suit, but pretty soon he said, "No, I'm still not like Dr. Lee." He said, "Well, if I can't dress like, I'll baptize like him." He had seen Dr. Lee baptize and the ordinance of baptism so beautifully portrayed as Dr. Lee buried the candidate and symbolically brought him up from the water. He tried to do that and nearly drowned his candidates. One night he came home from church and asked, "Honey, make me an onion sandwich."

"An onion sandwich? Why on earth do you want an onion sandwich?"

He answered, "Well, when Dr. Lee gets through preaching on Sunday night, he goes home, sits down at the kitchen table, and his wife makes him an onion sandwich; and if I can't preach like him, if I can't dress like him, if I can't baptize like him, I'm gonna smell like him!"

I can't be Dr. Lee, and you can't be Dr. Lee, but you are the only person who can be what God has called you to be. I learned that I was appointed in the plan of God. Jesus said, "[God has] appointed me" (Luke 22:29).

Then I learned when my life and ministry turned the corner that I was anointed by the power of God. Jesus said, "The Spirit of the Lord is upon me, for he hath anointed me to preach the gospel" (Luke 4:18). Then He told about five groups of people whose lives would be changed when the gospel was preached. He talked about the blind, the beggars, the bruised, the bound, and I have discovered that God has anointed us. God does not appoint us without providing the anointing of His Spirit to carry out His will and plan for our lives. Paul said to the Thessalonians, "For our gospel came not unto you in word only, but also in power, and in the Holy

Ghost, and in much assurance" (1 Thess. 1:5). How wonderful, and what a comfort it is to know that the power is not mine. It does not depend on my ability; it does not depend on my talent; it does not depend on what I can do, but it depends on my reliance upon the Holy Spirit who has anointed me to preach the gospel that is the power of God unto salvation. If anything is going to happen, it is going to happen because of the anointing of God upon my life. I love that old hymn we sing:

> Brethren, we have met to worship
> And adore the Lord our God;
> Will you pray with all your power
> While we try to preach the Word?
> All is vain, unless the Spirit
> Of the Holy One comes down.

I learned all is vain unless the Spirit of God comes down. I discovered that God had already poured out His spirit. God had already provided me the anointing of His Spirit. We pray for another Pentecost, and I know what we mean by that. We mean, "God, do a mighty work in us as you did at Pentecost." We don't need to pray for another Pentecost any more than we need to pray for another Calvary. If I got up today and said, "I've sinned and I need to be saved, Jesus come and die on the cross for our sins," Brother Sam Cathey would say, "You don't need to pray that way, He has already died for your sins. You need to believe that He has died for your sins and enter into Calvary." Instead of praying for another Pentecost, we need to realize that God has already poured out His Spirit and believe that He has poured out His Spirit in our lives and confess our sins and have our vessels cleansed and claim by faith the filling of His Spirit. I learned that I was anointed by the Spirit of God and the power of God in my life.

I heard about a young boy who went off to one of these fancy, expensive colleges. Boy, the bills were coming in! One day his mother received a letter from him, and he wrote, "I have failed all of my courses. I'm coming home, prepare Dad." She wrote a letter back to him and just said, "Dad is prepared. Prepare yourself."

God showed me that He was prepared. God showed me that it was not a matter of my waiting on God. God was waiting on me. God was saying, "When are you going to understand? I've provided everything you need." Romans 8:37 says, "We are more than conquerors through him that loved us." Preachers, do we preach like we are more than conquerors? The Bible doesn't say we will be—it says we are! That means that we are super conquerors. Paul, in essence, says, "There is not a word in my vocabulary to adequately describe the victory we have in Jesus." We are more than conquerors.

Most Christians and preachers act like it's just barely a victory for the believers. The believers, in the last thirty seconds of the football game, kick a field goal, and it's the believers 21 and the devil 18. We just barely won. Paul, the apostle, says, "No, it's the believers 90, the devil 0!" "We are more than conquerors through him that loved us."

I heard about that fellow who came into town to a Little League baseball game. He looked at the scoreboard, 21 to 0. A little boy was sitting on the bench while his team was in the field. The other team was batting, and the fellow said to the little boy on the bench, "Son, it looks pretty bad for your team."

The little boy replied, "Oh, no Sir, we haven't come up to bat yet!"

Sometimes it looks like the devil is winning. Sometimes it appears that Satan has the upper hand in our lives, in our ministry, in our world, but friend, we have to read the end of the book. We are more than conquerors. God has already anointed us with His power, and we need to enter into that experience and receive, by faith, what God has for us.

When my life and ministry turned the corner, I learned I was appointed, uniquely, in the plan of God, that God would use me. I learned that I was anointed by the power of God and as I preached the gospel, God would open the prison doors and free those who were enslaved by the devil, that God would give the beggars true riches of His grace, that God would open the eyes that had been blinded by the god of this world. God, through His anointed Word, preached through His servant.

Last of all, my life and ministry turned the corner when I learned that *spiritual achievement comes through appropriating the promises of God*. God wants to be so much in our lives, and we are content with so little. We look at someone's ministry who is baptizing many people or someone in whose life unusual things are happening, and, as preachers, we want to say, "Well, it's because he knows the right people, or it's because he's bringing in all the bus kids and baptizing them, or it's because he's got a gimmick. He's giving away Shetland ponies."

We want to figure out what God is doing, but in most cases, I discovered that the secret is: here is a man who has learned to believe God for great things. Here is a man who has learned that he is appointed by the plan of God, anointed by the power of God, and he can appropriate the promises of God, and God will do what He says. Jesus said, "All things are possible to him that believeth" (Mark 9:23). The Bible says, "Now unto him who is able to do exceedingly, abundantly above all that we ask or think" (Eph. 3:20). God said, "You can't outthink me, you can't out ask me, you can't out plan me, you can't out drain me." God says, "It's a blank check." Why don't we appropriate the promises of God in our lives, all that God has planned to do?

I've learned that I could appropriate the promises of God in the midst of failure. There are times when I have failed in preaching a sermon. There are times when I made a mistake in the planning of a program. There are so many mistakes and so many plans that have gone wrong and so many times I have failed God. But I have learned that when I repent of my sins and put my eyes on the Lord Jesus Christ that, in spite of failure, God picks me up and says, "You are my man, appointed in my plan, anointed with my power, and you have my promise, and you don't need anything else."

When I was a boy at Sweetwater I liked to play baseball. I played by myself. I went out there and took the bat and threw the ball up, and just got after it. I heard about a little fellow who did that one day. He threw the ball up the first time and tried to hit it—strike one! He said, "Now look, I'm a baseball star, I'll get it on the second try." He threw it up again—strike two! Well, he picked it up a third time. He said, "Three strikes in baseball." He picked it up, threw it high, watched it carefully, and then swung with all of his might, but he missed it. He threw the bat down and said, "Boy! What a pitcher I am." Appropriate the promises, in spite of failure. Edmund Vance Cooke wrote:

> What is failure?
> It is only a spur within the one who receives it,
>   right?
> To make the spirit in him want to go out and fight
> If you've never failed, it's an easy guess
> You've never been a great success.

The great men of God are not those who have never failed; they are those who have failed and failed and failed until they decided and were determined to appropriate God's promises, depending on God and relying on God and trusting God. One of our problems is that when we fail we don't look to Jesus.

Jonah failed, but he wasn't a failure. He came back and preached one of the greatest revivals in recorded history. Peter failed when he first denied the Lord, but he wasn't a failure. He came back and, anointed by the Spirit of God, he preached on the Day of Pentecost, and 3,000 souls were saved. John Mark failed when he let Paul down, and he said, "I'm going back. I'm not going to serve anymore," but he wasn't a failure. He came back and God used him. Jacob failed when he lied, when he went back on his vows for God, when he went into idolatry, but he wasn't a failure. He came back to wrestle with God and depend on God, and he became a prince in Israel. We may fail, but I've learned that failure does not keep us from appropriating the promises of God. We pick ourselves up, we dust ourselves off, and we say, "We are going to rely on all that God has for us."

Then I learned that we can achieve through the promises of God in spite of fatigue. Has there been a time when so many preachers are as tired as they are today and so many Christians as defeated. We've made so many hospital visits and we've made so many prospect visits and we've gone this way and that way and we've done this and that until we have today what is called "ministerial burnout"; preachers who say, "I can't preach anymore. I can't serve anymore, I can't plan another program. I can't have another revival meeting. I'm tired of it. I don't have any more strength." Your strength is in God and when you come to the place you don't have strength, Paul says, "When I am weak, then I am strong" (2 Cor. 12:10). When I come to the place when I'm fatigued, then I can achieve and appropriate the promises of God. When God doesn't do it, it won't be done. Isaiah wrote, "They that wait upon the Lord shall renew their strength; They shall mount up with wings as eagles. They shall run and not be weary; and they shall walk, and not faint" (40:31). God will supply the strength you need.

God said, "Stan, you are appointed in My plan. You are anointed with the power of God, and here are all the promises of God. Now, Son, go out there and claim it."

When Napoleon was making his march and had never tasted defeat, his troops came into the Alps and met and grappled with the enemy, Napoleon stood on a high vantage point, looked down on the battleground below, and saw his troops losing the battle. He saw his men being routed, and he said to the little bugle boy, "Blow the retreat, Son. If our troops don't fall back, all will be lost. They are being defeated, and we are going to be totally overthrown. Blow the retreat."

The little bugle boy, with a puzzled look upon his face, replied, "Sir, I don't know how to blow a retreat!"

Napoleon commanded, "Son, blow the retreat. It's imperative. Do it immediately."

The boy repeated, tears coursing down his cheeks, "But Sir, I don't know how. I've never blown a retreat."

Napoleon demanded, "Son, you blow that retreat the best you can."

The little boy took his bugle, put it up to his lips, and began to blow with all his might. Try though he might, the sound that came out was not a retreat, but that of a victorious charge ringing out over that valley. When Napoleon's troops heard it they thought their fellow soldiers were coming up from the ranks to help them. The enemy heard and thought that Napoleon had reinforcements coming down upon them, and they began to fall back. Napoleon's troops began to advance, and that day a resounding victory was won for France because one little bugler did not know how to blow a retreat.

God is going to use men and women who, because of the power of God, the plan of God, and the promises of God in their lives, never learned how to blow a retreat!

7

Foundation for Fruitfulness

Now when they heard this, they were pricked in their heart, and said unto Peter and to the rest of the apostles, Men and brethren, what shall we do?

Then Peter said unto them, Repent, and be baptized every one of you in the name of Jesus Christ for the remission of sins, and ye shall receive the gift of the Holy Ghost.

For the promise is to you, and to your children, and to all that are afar off, even as many as the Lord our God shall call.

And with many other words did he testify and exhort, saying, Save yourselves from this untoward generation.

Acts 2:37-40

In Acts 2, we have the record of the Day of Pentecost. How would you like to be in a service where 3,000 souls were saved? I believe this is a number God has put in His Word for a purpose and for a reason, showing His mighty power. I'd like to be in that kind of a service, and that is what happened on the Day of Pentecost. It occurred after they had witnessed and shared in the power of the Holy Spirit. People had fallen under conviction, and the gospel had been clearly presented.

I recently counseled with a young couple about to be married. I asked both of them, as I do with every engaged couple, to give me their testimony about their experience with the Lord Jesus. The young lady talked about her experience, about how she was saved in a Baptist church, and how wonderful it was to have Christ in her heart. Then she told me about how her parents had divorced and how it seemed that, because of the divorce, no one really cared, and that her parents had really lost interest in whether or not she was in church. She confessed that she dropped out and didn't grow, and hadn't been growing, but that she had been coming to San Jacinto, and God was working in her life again.

The young man admitted he had never received Christ as his Savior. I asked him if anyone had ever shown him how to invite Jesus into his heart, and he said that no one ever had. I asked him if he would allow me to share with him how Jesus could come into his life because, I pointed out, that if he was going to get married, the basis of his marriage had to be Christ, and that was the most important counsel I could share with him. He let me share with him the gospel of Jesus Christ, and he invited Christ to come into his heart and life.

So many times we feel that because we have heard salvation again and again and again that people everywhere know about salvation, but the fact is that masses of people do not understand what it means to be born again, what it means to be saved, and to receive Christ into their lives.

Some people think that to be saved is just joining the church. Some people think to be saved is just being baptized. Others think to be saved is for people to live a good life. There are some folks who think they are saved because they are Texans! They have these stickers on the back of their trucks, and I think that is fine, and I'm glad that I'm living in Texas, but being a Texan does not make you a child of God.

Before you can be a child of God, before you can miss hell and go to heaven, there has to be God's part, and God's part is to call you to salvation. You cannot be saved until God's Spirit calls you and God calls us in two ways. (1) God calls us through the Scriptures, and (2) God calls us through the Spirit. Nobody is saved apart from the Word of God. God calls people through the preaching, teaching, and sharing of His Word. Paul said, "I am not ashamed of the gospel of Christ: for it is the power of God unto salvation" (Rom. 1:16). God's Word is the power.

I believe the Bible is the Word of God. I'm grateful that I'm in a church of people who believe the Bible is the Word of God. I believe the Bible from Genesis to maps! All of it is the Word of God, and God calls people to salvation through His Word. When Simon Peter preached on the Day of Pentecost, again and again he quoted the Word of God. He quoted the Psalms, the prophets, the Old Testament Scriptures, and it was the Word of God being proclaimed and preached that began to prepare the hearts of those 3,000 people who were going to be saved and find Christ as their Lord and Savior. The Bible says that, "Faith cometh by hearing, and hearing by the word of God" (Rom. 10:17). That's why it is so important for us to get people under the sound of the gospel of Jesus Christ.

I was walking into the hospital one day when a lady stopped me and said, "I know you are not here to see me or my husband—he's in intensive care—but I want you to know that he was saved listening to you preach over television, and if he doesn't make it out of this hospital, I know he'll be in heaven." It's not Stan Coffey who calls anybody to salvation. It's the preaching of the Word of God. There is something about the Word of God that prepares people's hearts. There is a power and a built-in conviction when people hear this Word preached. The Bible says, "My word . . . shall not return unto me void" (Isa. 55:11).

Not only must there be God's call through the Scriptures, there is also God's call through the Spirit. The Bible says, "Now when they heard this, they were pricked in their heart" (v. 37). That word "pricked" means to be pricked as with a sharp knife. I mean being stabbed in their hearts. That means when God's Spirit spoke to them. When God's Spirit convicted them deep down inside, all of a sudden they realized they were sinners. They realized they were on their way to hell. They recognized that the Bible wasn't just a bunch of stories, but the Bible was true, and they became aware that they had crucified Jesus. They had put Jesus on that cross. It says, "When they heard this, they were pricked in their heart." What did they hear? He said, "Therefore let all of the house of Israel know assuredly, that God hath made that same Jesus, whom ye have crucified, both Lord and Christ" (v. 36).

I can remember when I was saved. One of the things that brought me to Jesus was that the Spirit of God showed me Calvary and how Jesus died for my sins. I remember the preacher in that revival meeting talking about the cross and the question that Pilate asked, "[What will I do with] Jesus who is called Christ?" (Matt. 27:17, NASB). He explained how Jesus had died for me, how He bled for me, and how He rose again for me. Then he asked the question, "What will you do with Jesus?" I determined that night, "I'm going to trust Him."

If you feel you've sinned against God, if God shows you that you need to be saved, it's not the preacher, it's not a friend, but it's the Spirit of the living God Who is speaking to your heart. If you have the slightest desire to come to Christ, it is because of the work of the Holy Spirit. The Bible says that when "he is come he will reprove the world of sin and of righteousness and of judgment" (John 16:9). Sometimes people will remark when they walk out of the church, "Man, you really stepped on my toes today." I didn't stop on anybody's toes. The Spirit of God took His Word and applied it to their hearts, and the Spirit of God is in the business of stepping on toes. If I went to a church where my toes were never stepped on, I'd wonder whether or not the truth was really being preached because the truth, the Word of God, is like a sharp, two-edged sword. The Spirit takes that sword, and He pricks our hearts. He breaks our hearts over sin and shows us we are wrong and that we are on the road to hell. He reveals to us that the lake of fire is real and that we are headed there. We are lost in our sin without Jesus Christ, and we realize the only thing that can help us is by coming and bowing at the foot of the cross and giving our lives to Jesus our Savior. That is the call of the Spirit.

There is also mankind's part. God will do His part, but what is man's part? Man's part, in salvation, is fourfold. One, in order to be saved there must be repentance of sin. They said, "Men and brethren, what shall we do?" (v. 37). He didn't say anything about joining the church, about living a good life, or about "doing the best you can." He said, "Repent, [Repent, Repent]" (v. 38). Jesus said, "Except ye repent, ye shall all likewise perish" (Luke 13:3,5). Why do I know some members of San Jacinto Baptist Church who are on their way to the lake of fire? Because they have never repented of their sins. They have never been convicted that they were lost, and the problem with some of them is not that they need to be saved but, first of all, they need to be lost! Some of them have never realized that they are lost, that hell is real, and they they are on their way to hell without Jesus Christ, and they cannot be saved until first they realize they are lost and without Christ.

They have to be convicted of sin in order to repent from sin. Repent is a military term which means about-face. Sin means walking away from God, walking in your own way, doing what you want to do, and saying, "It's my life, and I'll live it. I don't want any parents, I don't want any pastor, I don't want any Sunday School teacher telling me what to do. I'll live my own life." But when you repent, the Bible indicates that you do an about-face and go in the opposite direction. You go toward God, toward Christ, toward heaven, toward the things of the Spirit, toward the Word of God. That's repentance. Repentance is a change of direction and attitude. It means a change of attitude about yourself, your sins, your way of thinking about the Lord and His will and His purpose and His grace for your life. You change your attitude toward God.

I've noticed that when people repent, their attitude is the first thing to change, and when their attitude changes, when their mind changes, their life begins to change. They become a new person, a new creation in Christ. I look at many people who claim to be Christians, and they claim to believe in Jesus, but the problem is: I've never seen a change of attitude. I've never seen repentance in their lives, and "unless you repent, ye shall all likewise perish." There has to be that change of attitude toward God which confesses, "God, I've been going my way, but now I want to go your way."

It also means a change of Lord. It means that no longer are you on the throne of your life, but now Jesus is on that throne. By an act of your will, you say, "Lord Jesus, I want You to be my Lord." The Bible says, "If you confess with your mouth Jesus as Lord . . ." (Rom. 10:9, NASB). Many people don't understand this. They think salvation is a cafeteria line where you say, "I'll have Saviorhood, please, but no lordship, thank you." They simply want to take what they want. "I'll take eternal life, but I don't want discipleship."

Don't you be deceived. Jesus Christ does not come into your life to be Savior only. You can't divide Jesus Christ. Jesus is called in the Bible, "The Lord Jesus Christ."

What is the emphasis of Scripture? The emphasis of Scripture is not that Jesus is some fire insurance from hell. The emphasis of Scripture is that Jesus wants to come in to be Boss, Owner, Lord, Master of your life, to call the shots in your life, to change your life. Many people claim to be Christians. They say, "He's my Savior," but they know nothing about lordship. They talk the way they want to talk, live the way they want to live, do what they want to do, have the friends they want to have, and go the way they want to go. Jesus is not Lord of their life.

Some people say, "Well, I accepted Jesus as Savior when I was twelve, and then I made Him the Lord of my life when I was twenty-five." Well, as far as the Bible is concerned, there's no way you could accept Jesus as Savior and be saved, have eternal life, and be on your way to heaven unless you also receive Him as your Lord. He is the *Lord* Jesus Christ! If He is not your Lord, He is not your Savior.

So many preachers are busy expounding positive thinking, positive living, possibility thinking, and all the rest that there is little preaching about the lordship of Jesus Christ. But Peter emphasized that you have to make Him Lord. God has highly exalted Him and given Him a name that is above every name, and you're going to bow before Him one day. If you are going to be saved, you're going to bow before Him now.

If He is your Lord, are you doing what He commands? If He is your Lord, are you following Him, day by day? There has to be repentance of sin.

Then there must be the reception of the Spirit. He says,

"Ye shall receive the gift of the Holy Ghost" (v. 38). Now, not the gifts of the Holy Ghost, but "the gift of the Holy Ghost." "The gift of the Holy Ghost" means the Holy Spirit Himself. It means God, the third Person of the Trinity, comes to live in your heart. God indwells you. He comes in to be your personal Savior and Lord. "The gift of the Holy Spirit" is distinguished from *the gifts* of the Spirit. The gifts of the Spirit are those abilities and those supernatural endowments of motivation that God gives to each member of the body as He will. The gift of the Spirit is His indwelling. He indwells every child of God. Every child of God has the Holy Spirit. That's why John said in his first letter, "[This is the way we know we are children of God.] Hereby know we that we dwell in him, and he in us, because he hath given us of his Spirit" (John 4:13). The Bible says that His Spirit bears witness with our spirit that we are children of God (see Rom. 8:16). It means that there will be a confirming in your spirit by His Spirit that you are a child of God. One of the greatest ways to know that you are saved is the internal witness God gives you when you say, "I am a child of God." There's a confirmation in your spirit, given to you by the Holy Spirit.

If you are a child of God, biblical salvation means the reception of the Spirit. That's what it means to be born again. God's Spirit takes up residence and makes your spirit alive unto God.

Next, there is the response of baptism. "Repent, and be baptized, every one of you in the name of Jesus Christ for the remission of sins" (v. 38). Baptism is not optional. We as Baptists, in order to steer away from the doctrine of baptismal regeneration, the false belief that water baptism saves, have deemphasized baptism historically. Baptism is not deemphasized in the Book of Acts, however. Everytime anybody was saved in the Book of Acts, they were always baptized. There is no exception to it. Baptism is not optional. You cannot be an obedient child of God and refuse to be baptized, because it is a command of our Lord. Baptism is mandatory. God commanded it for every person who would follow Jesus Christ. I believe there is no way a person who is truly saved can refuse to be baptized. Baptism was so important to Jesus that He walked over seventy miles in order to be baptized in water. Some say, "Brother Stan, is it really that important for me to get into that baptistry and follow Jesus?" It was very important to Jesus, and He set the example for us.

Jesus was baptized and the Father said from heaven, "This is my beloved Son in whom I am well pleased" (Matt. 4:17). It pleases God today for you to come and request, "I want to be baptized."

Baptism is to follow salvation; it is never to precede it. It's not "be baptized and believe." It's not "be baptized and repent." It's "repent and be baptized." It's "believe and be baptized." Some people have the order wrong. One of our fine deacons came recently to say, "I've got the order wrong. I made a decision when I was young and thought I was saved. Later on I realized that I was not saved. I gave my life to Christ, and I know exactly when my life began to change. I know exactly when God came into my life but since that time, I haven't been baptized, and I need to get the order right." If you went under that water before you were saved, and you haven't been baptized after you were saved, you just got wet. You don't have Scriptural baptism. Scriptural baptism is being baptized *because of your belief, because of your salvation, because you've been converted.*

What does this mean, "Be baptized . . . for the remission of sins"? The King James uses the word *for*. It is from the Greek word *eis;* and we use the word *for* in English like they used it in Greek. What does it mean? It can mean in order to, because of, or in reference to. What does it mean here? Is He saying, "Repent and be baptized in order to have your sins forgiven," or is He saying, "Repent and be baptized because your sins have been forgiven"? When I attended college, I went for an education. When I graduated, I wept for joy, not because I wanted to obtain joy but because I had joy. That's what it means here. It means to be baptized *because* your sins have been forgiven. The moment you come to Christ, your sins are forgiven. You are cleansed by the blood of the cross of Calvary. You are made a new person; you are born again by the Spirit of God. Then you are baptized, buried with Him in baptism, to give testimony to the fact that you have been saved, that your sins have been forgiven. As Christ died and was buried, even so we should rise and walk in newness of life as He was raised from the dead (Rom. 6:4). That's why you are baptized.

One little boy in our bus ministry was saved, and the bus captain advised him, "Now, I want you to go to the 'big church,' and when the preacher gives the invitation, I want you to come down the aisle and tell him you've been saved and want to be baptized."

The boy said, "OK." He went forward and said, "I've been saved, and I want to get advertised."

Some people think he was wrong, but I believe he was right. It's advertising the fact that you love Jesus, that you are obedient to Him, that you have followed Him. That's why we always baptize at the end of every service. Many times those who are baptized have been counseled in the homes, and they've made that decision, and baptism has been explained. Many times the Spirit of God has fallen on them in the service, and they want to be obedient to Christ. But did you notice the Bible says that the same day there were added unto them 3,000 souls? Baptism, in the New Testament, was always immediate. You find nothing in the New Testament where people had a waiting period for baptism, where they waited, took a study course, and then were baptized. I assure you: if the Holy Ghost convicts you and you are saved, you are ready to be baptized. You don't have to learn the Book of Revelation. You don't have to learn Baptist doctrine. You don't have to learn one other truth because baptism is the first act of discipleship.

Through my ministry, I have noticed that people who followed Christ in baptism as soon as possible after they were saved, stayed with it, made better disciples, and had more confidence in their Christian life than people who did otherwise. As a matter of fact, I have seen cases where people did not grow in their Christian life for a long time because they put off their baptism.

Last, there is the renunciation of the world. He goes on to say that he exhorted and testified unto them with many other words, saying, "Be saved from this perverse generation!" (v. 40, NASB). There is only one way to be saved from the problems, the difficulties, and the challenges of this world. We are living in a world where Christians increasingly are in the minority, where AIDS is rampaging across the country, where drugs continue to eat away at the lives of young people and old, where the problems and stresses of life continue to destroy homes. There is only way to be saved from this perverse world, and that's to give your life to Jesus Christ. It is a warped, twisted generation. If his generation was perverse, what would Peter say about this one? Coming to Christ is the only way to build a life, to build a home, to build a career, to build a marriage. Come to Jesus Who said, "I am come that they might have life" (John 10:10). Jesus said, "Behold, I stand at the door, and knock: if any man hear my voice, and open the door, I will come in to him, and will sup with him, and he with me" (Rev. 3:20).

What is biblical salvation? It's hearing the call of the Scripture. It's hearing the call of the Spirit in your heart. It's knowing that Jesus is knocking at the door of your life. And it's opening that door and inviting Jesus to come in.

8

Preaching for Results

And they were all filled with the Holy Ghost . . .

But Peter, standing up with the eleven, lifted up his voice and said unto them, Ye men of Judaea and all ye that dwell at Jerusalem, be this known unto you and hearken to my words.

Ye men of Israel, hear these words; Jesus of Nazareth, a man approved of God among you by miracles and wonders and signs, which God did by him in the midst of you, as ye yourselves know:

Him being delivered by the determinate counsel and foreknowledge of God, ye have taken, and by wicked hands have crucified and slain:

Whom God hath raised up, having loosed the pains of death: because it was not possible that he should be holden of it.

Now when they heard this, they were pricked in their heart, and said unto Peter and to the rest of the apostles, Men and brethren, what shall we do?

Then Peter said unto them. Repent, and be baptized every one of you in the name of Jesus Christ for the remission of sins, and ye shall receive the gift of the Holy Ghost.

Acts 2:4*a*,14,22-24,37-38

Someone has suggested that a good pastor is one who preaches exactly twenty minutes and then sits down. He condemns sin but never hurts anyone's feelings. He labors from 8:00 AM to 10:00 PM in every kind of work from preaching to custodial services. He makes sixty dollars per week, wears good clothes, buys good books, has a nice family, drives a good car, and gives thirty dollars a week to the church. He also stands ready to contribute to every work that comes along.

The ideal pastor is twenty-six years old and has been preaching for thirty years. He is at once tall and short, thin and heavyset, and handsome. He has one brown eye and one blue eye. His hair is parted in the middle with the left side dark and straight and the right side brown and wavy. He has a burning desire to work with teenagers and spends all of his time with the older folk.

He smiles all of the time with a straight face because he has a sense of humor that keeps him seriously dedicated to his work. He makes fifteen calls a day on church members, spends all of his time evangelizing the unchurched, and is never out of his office.

Now this is a humorous description, but pastors and laymen alike know that many unrealistic demands are made on the pastor. The one demand we must listen to is that of the Lord who spoke through Paul in Ephesians 4, that the job of the pastor is to equip the saints for the work of ministry.

I believe that an important priority in equipping the saints is that every pastor must also be his own evangelist. I still believe that the greatest tool for evangelism today is the morning worship services of our churches.

Paul wrote to Timothy and challenged him, "Do the work of an evangelist" (2 Tim. 4:5). I am not saying that you shouldn't use full-time evangelists for revivals. God has given to the church gifted evangelists, and I use them. But every year I also preach at least one of San Jacinto's revivals, and every Sunday I include an evangelistic appeal within my regular Sunday message. That does not mean I always preach an entire message on the plan of salvation, but it does mean that every time I am before my people, I have the opportunity to do the work of an evangelist, to bring the message of the Good News of Christ, and to invite people to receive Him as Lord and Savior.

I do not believe we will ever have the kind of churches God wants until we realize He desires us to do the work of an evangelist and that the greatest tool we have is that of effective evangelistic preaching.

If there ever was a time when effective evangelistic preaching is needed, it is now. There is today an openness to the gospel. There is a responsiveness to the Holy Spirit, and there are unlimited opportunities for every pastor to be an evangelistic preacher. God did not intend for us to depend upon a revival crusade once or twice a year to be our means of evangelism. God intends that every preaching opportunity be used as a means of effective evangelistic preaching.

The best example of effective evangelistic preaching is found in Acts 2.

I. The Power for Evangelistic Preaching

In Acts 2:4, the Bible says, "And they were all filled with the Holy Spirit" (NASB).

Verse 14 says, "But Peter, standing up with the eleven, lifted up his voice and said unto them, Ye men of Judaea and all ye that dwell at Jerusalem, be this known unto you and hearken to my words."

I want you to notice this fact carefully. Peter did not stand up to preach before the coming of the Holy Spirit. He was empowered to preach only *after* he had been filled with the Spirit of God.

This word "filled" means Peter was "taken possession of" by the Holy Ghost. When Peter stood to preach, he was wholly and completely God's man. I would tell you today that until every part of our being—body, mind, and spirit—has been yielded and surrendered to God, we cannot preach effective evangelistic sermons.

How many times have you studied and prepared for a sermon, thinking you had created a literary gem, and you went to the pulpit to preach, but there was no fire of God, and nothing happened? The kind of preaching that brings people to Christ is preaching empowered by the Spirit of God.

Someone asked D. L. Moody how to revive a cold, dead congregation, and he replied, "Build a fire in the pulpit." One sage has suggested that the reason we have so many icebergs in the pews is that we have so many polar bears in the pulpit! When the Holy Spirit fills you and anoints you to preach, it is going to change the monotonous into the momentous.

We, as Baptists, have allowed the Pentecostals and charismatics to frighten us away from the doctrine of the Holy Spirit. We've been so afraid of wildfire that we settle for no fire. But the Bible teaches that there is, for every man of God, the provision of God to be filled with the Spirit and to be anointed by the Spirit to preach the Word of God.

In Acts 1:8, Jesus said, "Ye shall receive power after that the Holy Ghost has come upon you."

Think of it. The disciples who attended the greatest seminary on earth, with Jesus as the Founder, President, and Professor, were not yet ready for spiritual work until they had been filled with God's Holy Spirit. When we preach, depending upon our talent, our training, and our education, we will fail. But when we are filled with the Holy Spirit, we'll see the invisible; we'll know the unknowable; we'll do the impossible, and iron gates will yield before us, because it is not what we are doing, but what God is doing through us!

Whether or not we agree on every point, whether or not we come from the same school, the thing we all need is an old-fashioned baptism of the Holy Ghost's power upon our pulpits and upon our ministries.

The life of D. L. Moody intrigues me. I read of the time when he was in New York City. Moody was on Wall Street and while walking down that canyon of financial prestige, there was an unusual occurrence. Two ladies had been praying for God to do His powerful work in the life of D. L.

Moody, and Moody was all of a sudden so overcome by the power of the Holy Spirit that he fell on his face before God, asking God to withhold His hand until he could be alone. He went into the home of a friend, and God did a new work in his life. Moody testified that whereas he used to have five conversions, he would have one hundred conversions, preaching the same sermon. Mr. Moody knew for the first time that the supernatural power of the Holy Spirit had settled upon his life.

When I read that, I cried, "Oh, God, I wonder if what you had for D. L. Moody, you could have for Stan Coffey. I wonder if it could be that experience Moody had, that breath of God that came on Moody; the power that changed his ministry. Oh, God, do you think that power could be for me?"

I read the life of Savonarola. He went to the pulpit one Sunday and refused to preach. He sat there for an hour, and he still wouldn't preach. He decided, "I'll not preach until the power of God comes on me." He sat there for two hours while the anxious crowd waited. Through the third hour he sat; through the fourth hour he sat. For five hours, he sat on the platform and refused to preach.

But all of a sudden, the blessing and glory of God came on him, and the power of God was there, the power of the supernatural. That's what we need in evangelistic preaching, the anointing and the power of the Holy Spirit of God.

We need a generation of old-fashioned Holy Ghost-filled, Holy Ghost-led men of God who, when they speak, something happens in the hearts of people.

I read the life of Christmas Evans who was blinded the first day of his ministry because he was stoned by the crowd.

On his deathbed, he looked into the faces of young preachers and urged, "Young men, preach the blood," and he went to be with his Savior.

One day, Christmas Evans was riding his circuit. All of a sudden, the Holy Spirit of God shook him and knocked him off his horse. Evans fell on his face and, "For the first time," Evans testified, "I was filled with the Holy Spirit."

I read about John Wesley who, in an all-night prayer meeting at 3 o'clock one morning, knew for the first time what it was to be filled with the Holy Spirit.

I read about George Whitefield who knelt to be ordained. When Bishop Benson laid his hands on him, Whitefield said, "I so yielded myself to the Spirit of God that I knew it was the first time I had been filled with the Holy Spirit."

I read about Charles G. Finney who declared that the first day he was converted, he was filled with the Holy Spirit.

I'm not a Pentecostal. I have a Baptist head, a Pentecostal heart, and Jehovah's Witness feet. But I know this: When I read about those men and how God anointed their ministry, filled their ministry with the Holy Spirit, I say, "Oh, God of D. L. Moody; oh, God of Savonarola; oh, God of Charles Finney; oh, God of Evans and Wesley and Whitefield: fill me with your Holy Spirit. Anoint me to preach as I have never preached before." I believe we must have a supernatural anointing of God's power if we are to be the preachers we ought to be.

A preacher was discouraged. He went before his church that didn't seem to be growing and said, "I'm going to resign," and he went away to a conference on evangelism.

He arrived a little late, and all the seats were filled. A huge crowd had gathered. He leaned back against the wall, and he dropped his chin upon his chest. The preacher began to preach.

God began to speak to that preacher. He realized that God was greater than all of his opposition, greater than all his inabilities. He began to see how it would be possible for the power of God to so come upon him that his life would be a mighty instrument in the hands of God.

He stood there and wept as the Spirit of God searched deep down in his soul, and that night, standing against the wall, he prayed, "Dear Lord, if you'll give me another chance, If you'll stir my soul, if you'll clothe me with the power of God, I'll be an evangelistic preacher."

He sent a wire back to his little church which read about like this: "You're going to have a new preacher next Sunday. Be sure to be there to hear him."

The next Sunday morning, from all outward appearances, the same preacher walked to the pulpit, but he wasn't the same. He walked to that pulpit with a broken and burning heart. He walked to that pulpit weeping over sinners, and he has been winning them to Christ ever since.

My friends, there are not enough demons in hell—Satan doesn't have enough power to overcome the preacher who is fully consecrated and yielded to the Spirit of God. There is the power for evangelistic preaching; the power of the Holy Spirit.

II. The Person for Evangelistic Preaching

Ye men of Israel, hear these words; Jesus of Nazareth, a man approved of God among you by miracles and wonders and signs, which God did by him in the midst of you, as ye yourselves also know:

> Him being delivered by the determinate counsel and foreknowledge of God, ye have taken, and by wicked hands have crucified and slain:
>
> Whom God hath raised up, having loosed the pains of death: because it was not possible that he should be holden of it (Acts 2:22-24).

Peter goes on in verses 25-26 to describe the person and work of Christ as the only way of salvation. In verse 36, he climaxes his message with, "God hath made that same Jesus, whom ye have crucified, both Lord and Christ."

Peter preached Jesus Christ. Christ was the center and heart of his message and if we are to accomplish effective evangelistic preaching, this must be our pattern—to make Christ the center of that message.

Later, Peter and John were arrested and brought to trial because they were teaching and preaching the name of Jesus. If it were a crime to preach in the name of Jesus, would any of us be arrested?

When Peter preached, he emphasized, "I preach unto you Jesus." There are so many things we'd like to preach. We would like to campaign for a better social order. We would like to demonstrate our intellectual abilities. We would like to clean up the sorry moral mess this world is in, but effective evangelistic preaching is a message that centers in the person of Jesus Christ.

People will never be saved until we preach Jesus. "There is none other name under heaven given among men, whereby we must be saved" (Acts 4:12). And Jesus says, "And I, if I be lifted up, . . . will draw all men unto me" (John 12:32). And, like Peter, we must level with our people, "Let me tell you what Jesus has done. Let me preach Christ to you. Let me tell you about One who can change your life. Let me tell you about One Who can forgive any sin. Let me tell you about One who can give your life purpose and meaning."

Effective evangelistic preaching must center in the person of Jesus Christ. There shouldn't be a problem, because all you have to do is open the Bible anywhere, and Jesus steps out. It's all His story from Genesis to Revelation. The Old Testament promises, "Someone is coming." The Gospels say, "Someone has come." The Epistles say, "Someone is coming again." If you read the Bible and don't see Jesus, then you need to reread the Bible because it is all about Jesus Christ.

In Genesis, Jesus is the Promised Seed.
In Exodus, He is the Passover Lamb.
In Leviticus, He is the Scapegoat.
In Numbers, He is the Brazen Serpent.
In Deuteronomy, He is the Great Lawgiver.

In Joshua, He is the Prophet, Priest, and King.
In Judges, He is the Judge of all the earth.
In Ruth, He is the Kinsman-Redeemer.
In Samuel, He is the Anointer of Kings.
In Kings, He is the King of kings and Lord of lords.

In Chronicles, He is the Historian.
In Ezra, He is the Restorer of the Temple.
In Nehemiah, He is the Rebuilder of the Wall.
In Esther, He is the Savior of the Jews.
In Job, He is a Friend that sticks closer than a
    brother.

In Psalms, He is the Song of the Ages.
In Proverbs, He is the Wisdom of God.
In Ecclesiastes, He is the Great Preacher.
In the Song of Solomon, He is a Wonderful Lover.

In Isaiah, He is Wonderful, Counselor, the Mighty God, the Everlasting Father, the Prince of Peace.

In Lamentations, He is a Street Preacher.
In Jeremiah, He is the Weeping Prophet.
In Ezekiel, He is the Restorer of the people of God.
In Daniel, He is the Stone cut out without hands from the mountainside.
In Hosea, He is a spurned but forgiving husband.

And in the Minor Prophets, He is the Star rising in Bethlehem's sky.

In Matthew, He is the King of kings.
In Mark, He is the Suffering Servant.
In Luke, He is the Son of man.
In John, He is the Son of God.
In Acts, He is the Power of the Church.

In Romans, He is the Dynamite of the Gospel.
In Corinthians, He is the Transformer of the carnal nature.
In Galatians, He is the Rent Vale.
In Ephesians, He is the Heavenly One.
In Philippians, He is the All-sufficient One.

In Colossians, He is the Preeminent One.
In Thessalonians, He is our Coming Savior.
In Timothy, He is our Great Appearing God.
In Titus, He is our Blessed Hope
In Philemon, He is the Emancipator of all the wayward slaves

In Hebrews, He is the Best of all.
In James, He is True Religion.
In Peter's Epistles, He is the Rock of our salvation.
In John's Epistles, He is Our Assurance.

In Jude, He is the One Who is able to keep us from
falling.
In Revelation, He is the One seated on the white
horse coming back, leading His armies in victory.

III. There Is a Purpose for Evangelistic Preaching

Effective evangelistic preaching is preaching which calls
for a decision.

> Now when they heard this, they were pricked in their
> heart, and said unto Peter and to the rest of the apos-
> tles, Men and brethren, what shall we do?
> Then Peter said unto them, Repent, and be bap-
> tized every one of you in the name of Jesus Christ for
> the remission of sins, and ye shall receive the gift of the
> Holy Ghost (Acts 2:37-38).

You say the idea of an invitation at every service designed
to call people to repentance and faith in Christ is old-
fashioned? I say to you it is patterned after Pentecost.

Effective evangelistic preaching calls for an immediate
decision. Peter preached, "Repent." The word "repent"
means "to turn." It means a conversion. It means a change of
lords. Peter called on these men to turn from their rejection of
Christ to an acceptance of Him as Savior and Lord and to be
baptized as evidence of that decision.

In Chicago one night a large crowd of people gathered to
hear D. L. Moody preach, but he did not give an invitation.
He simply dismissed the crowd with prayer. That same night,
hundreds of those same people died in the Chicago fire.
Moody's heart was broken, and he sobbed, "Never again will
I preach without giving an invitation."

Do not be afraid to ask people to decide for Christ. They are eternity bound. Eternity is long; sin is black; hell is hot and real, but heaven can be theirs if they will receive Christ. We must realize that the invitation is the most important part of the message.

So many times preachers deal with the invitation as though it is merely tacked on as part of the sermon. Drawing the net should be the most well-prepared part of the message, yet at this point most preachers fail.

There have been revivals in which some of the outstanding preachers of the world have preached to overflow audiences night after night with only two or three conversions, and then there are ministries in which mediocre preachers have consistently seen dozens of conversions week after week.

The difference: The power of the Spirit? Yes. Preparation? Yes. The power of God? Yes. The only big physical difference is that all-important phase of the ability to give an invitation.

Extending an invitation is the greatest agony in the ministry. We live and die a thousand deaths in the ten or twenty minutes in which the invitation is extended. Now when souls stand between life and death, we must be most dependent upon the Holy Spirit and most sensitive to His leadership.

An invitation extended too long may harden some heart that can never again be touched, but an invitation prematurely closed may miss that one last soul that was going to come on the next verse. I do not presume to be an authority on how to give an invitation, and yet there are some constant factors that God has used in my own ministry in this business of giving the invitation.

1. *Give the invitation with authority.*—Your frame of

mind, your attitude, your approach to it is of utmost importance. If you approach the invitation hesitantly with a note of apology, you might as well not give it at all.

Don't hesitate; don't apologize for it; just give it. The preacher's attitude is important, for the man in the pew can read your attitude. Remember, you have the authority of heaven behind you. Do not let criticism about a so-called "high-pressure" invitation defeat you at this point. Set your invitation on fire. If you don't believe it, they won't believe it.

Give your invitation with authority. Stand up with every bit of compassion the Spirit can give you, with every ounce of energy in your body, with sincerity in your voice, with a broken heart, inviting men, women and young people to turn from their sins and put their faith and trust in Jesus Christ.

2. *Give your invitation clearly.*—Never assume that the lost person knows what you want him to do. Many do not. Many times we ask, "Who will come for baptism?" or "Who will come for salvation?" or "Who will come by statement?" or "Who will come by letter?"

The average person doesn't know letter from better; or position from profession. Spell out exactly what you want them to do. Explain, step by step, that if they are willing to change their way of life, confess their sins, make Christ the Lord and Master of their lives, that you want them to step out to the nearest aisle, walk forward, and take you by the hand. Explain to them that they do not have to say anything, that their very act of coming means they are receiving Christ as Savior. Of course, when they come, you will counsel with them, pray with them, and deal with them properly. Make it as simple for them as you can possibly make it.

3. *Give the invitation positively.*—Never say, "If you are

going to come," but say, "As you come, I'll be here at the front to greet you and to help you in every way I can." Never plant a negative thought. Always assume they will come, and you expect them to come, and things are ready for them to come.

Step down from the pulpit and walk out down the aisle a few steps toward them. Let your gestures show expectancy. Let your face show expectancy. Let the tone of your voice be expectant.

One of Spurgeon's students complained, "Mr. Spurgeon, when I preach, I do not have decisions, but I notice that when you preach, you always have decisions."

Spurgeon then asked the student, "Young man, do you expect to have decisions every time you preach?"

The young man said, "Well, no." Spurgeon said, "That's why you don't have them."

I am afraid that many of us do not allow the Spirit of God to work because we do not expect anything to happen when we preach. We do not know the hearts of men. We do not know who in our congregation may be lost and may be having a struggle in his soul. So we need to expect God to work and move—and expect decisions every time we preach.

I expect decisions every Sunday morning, every Sunday night, and every Wednesday night. I used to overlook the Wednesday service, and I've discovered that it, too, can be an opportunity to invite people to Christ.

Peter told those people exactly what he wanted them to do. He said, "I want you to repent of your sins and as a sign that you have repented of your sins, I want you to follow Jesus Christ in believer's baptism." He gave an invitation authoritatively, clearly, and expectantly, and God gave him 3,000 souls.

Years ago, the first transoceanic cable message came from the King of England to the waiting hearts of millions of Americans. Seconds before the broadcast, the engineer discovered that the cable had been broken. Traumatically grasping both ends of the cable in his hands for twenty-seven minutes, the engineer allowed the message of the king to flow through his body to the nation. In exactly that way, every time we stand to give an invitation, we allow ourselves to be channels through which the Spirit of Christ flows into the hearts of waiting sinners.

Every pastor must do the work of the evangelist. His greatest opportunity is the pulpit ministry in his local church. If we are to be effective evangelistic preachers, then we must preach in the power of the Holy Spirit; our messages must center in the person of Christ; and our purpose must be to call people to decision.

9
Moving Toward Maximum Ministry

Now therefore fear the Lord, and serve him in sincerity and in truth: and put away the gods which your fathers served on the other side of the flood, and in Egypt; and serve ye the Lord.

And if it seem evil unto you to serve the Lord, choose you this day whom ye will serve; whether the gods which your fathers served that were on the other side of the flood, or the gods of the Amorites, in whose land ye dwell: but as for me and my house, we will serve the Lord.

And the people answered and said, God forbid that we should forsake the Lord, to serve other gods;

For the Lord our God, he it is that brought us up and our fathers out of the land of Egypt, from the house of bondage, and which did those great signs in our sight, and preserved us in all the way wherein we went, and among all the people through whom we passed:

And the Lord drave out from before us all the people, even the Amorites which dwelt in the land: therefore will we serve the Lord; for he is our God.

And Joshua said unto the people, Ye cannot serve

the Lord: for he is an holy God; he is a jealous God; he will not forgive your transgressions nor your sins.

If ye forsake the Lord, and serve strange gods, then he will turn and do you hurt, and consume you, after that he hath done you good.

And the people said unto Joshua, Nay; but we will serve the Lord.

Joshua 24:14-21

In Joshua 24, Joshua has come to the end of his ministry. God has sent him to lead the people of Israel into the Promised Land. Moses brought them out of Egypt, but Joshua led them into the Promised Land.

You remember that the Book of Joshua is about possessing our possessions, being all God wants us to be, possessing that which God has given to us. Now they have, for some years, been in the land conquering their enemies; and yet there remains much land to be possessed. They've not completed what God sent them into the land to do.

They've achieved many things. They've won many battles. They've had many trophies to show, and yet God speaks to them through Joshua and gives them the greatest challenge of their lives at the end of his ministry. God challenges the people and He says to them, in essence, "I want you to go on and be all God wants you to be. I don't want you to stop where you are." You see, they had conquered many parts of the land. They could have decided, "We are going to settle down now. We've done enough now. We have achieved many things, and many of our goals have come to pass. We have seen many dreams become a reality." They could have said, "We are going to stay right where we are," but God speaks to them through Joshua and challenges them to resist the temptation to become comfortable; to resist the temptation of mediocrity, to resist the temptation of being satisfied, and he says, "God doesn't want you just to rest on the laurels of the past. God wants you to continue on."

As Joshua reminds the people of all the good blessings of God, he tells them in this whole chapter, in the background, how God delivered from the land of Egypt and saved them with His mighty hand. He reminds them of the goodness of God, the blessings of God, the way God has continued to work in their lives, and then he challenges them, "But God is not finished with you yet. You have not come to the place of full maturity. You have not taken all the land." And so he says to them, in effect, "Don't be satisfied with where you are. Go on, and be all God wants you to be."

The reason I chose this text was because it reminded me of exactly where San Jacinto Baptist Church was. God has blessed us in so many wonderful ways. God has blessed us in the winning of souls to Christ, in the erection of buildings, and in the reaching of people through His mighty Spirit. We are at a place where it would be very easy for us to say, "Our buildings are full. We have reached their capacity. God has provided our needs. Now let's just enjoy what God has done." If we wanted to do what was easy; if we wanted to follow the line of least resistance, if we wanted to be self-satisfied, then we could alibi, "Let's just stay where we are." The decision that we face in our hearts, as individuals and as a church family, is: Are we going to settle for mediocrity? Are we going to settle for the status quo or are we going to go on and claim all of our possessions?

So many times we stop short of what God wants to do *in* us and what God wants to do *through* us. It is so easy to say, "Lord, You've been good to us here, and, God, You've blessed us here, You've prospered us here. We know what you are going to do here. God, we want to stay right where we are and praise you and worship you and serve you here. God, we want to settle for what we have now because we know exactly where we are. God, we know we can handle where we are. We know that we can achieve where we are and, Father, we just want to stay right where we are."

It's like that in your Christian life, isn't it? You reach a plateau in your Christian life where things are going well, where you're not having any particular problems, where you are enjoying your Christian life, where you've learned some things that have helped you to walk day by day, day in, day out. It is so tempting to say, "I am not going to go any further." That is where the average Christian is today. That is where the average Baptist church is today. They are what they are because they have chosen not to go beyond where they are.

Baptists program themselves to be a certain size, to accomplish certain things, and then they sit down and say, "That's enough, that's all we're going to do. That's all we need to do. God has been good. Let's just rejoice in the blessings and stay where we are. It's the safe thing to do. It's the sane thing to do." But God continually comes to His people as He did to those people and says, "Don't be satisfied." He says, "Don't stay where you are." God says, "Don't settle for less than I want to do through you." God says, "Don't settle for what I've done in the past. Go on and become all that I want you to be."

I believe God is challenging many people today. I believe many have stayed at a certain level. They have stayed on a certain plateau, and there they have ended their commitment. There they have ended what they are going to do. There they have ended what they are willing to expend for the cause of Christ, and they say, "Well, I'm better than most church members. I'm better than most Christians. God has used my life, and I'm going to stay right here."

I believe it's time that we hear the voice of God urging many of us, "I want you to go on." We need to hear the call of Johnson Oatman, Jr. who wrote, "I'm pressing on the upward way, New heights I'm gaining ev'ry day; Still praying as I onward bound, 'Lord plant my feet on higher ground.'" The church that doesn't hear that, and the Christian who doesn't hear that call and respond to it, is not only going to stay where he is, but he is going to begin to retreat in the Christian life.

When God asks us to go on, He never asks us to go without something to base our going on. I want you to understand why God says that we should go on to maturity; why we should possess all of our possessions and claim all the promises of God.

First of all, God says, "I want you to go on based on my demonstration of care." He says, "And I have given you a land for which ye did not labour, and cities which ye built not, and ye dwell in them; of the vineyards and oliveyards which ye planted not do ye eat" (v. 13). Now God says, "Based on My demonstration of care for you in the past, you should not be afraid of going on for Me." Notice there is a threefold thing that God says expressed His demonstration of care.

God says, first of all, "Based on My *prosperity*," second, "Based on My *protection*," and third, "Based on My *provision*." I challenge you to climb off the plateau that you've been on, and go on and be everything God has called you to be.

First of all, He said, "Based upon the way I have prospered you." He said, "I have given you a land for which ye did not labour" (v. 13*a*). Land represents prosperity. Land represents wealth. God said, "I have given you a land for which you did not labour." They had land to graze cattle on; land to graze sheep on, land to build houses on. Each of them had an inheritance. Every family of those who stayed faithful to God and went into the Promised Land had what they called a lot. That lot was their inheritance. God prospered them wonderfully. God said, "Based on the way I've loved you and prospered you, I challenge you to go and be what I want you to be."

God has prospered us. Why should we be afraid to go on when we consider how God has prospered us? Just look at your own life. Think about where you were ten years ago, fifteen years ago, twenty years ago. Think about where you are today. Look at the unbelievable manner in which God has prospered you and your family. Many people, if twenty years ago or even fifteen or ten years ago would have been told they would have what they have today in material possessions, would not have been able to believe it. We talk about being poor. We talk about being in need when we are living in a land of plenty and prosperity. God has blessed America. God has prospered this nation beyond any nation history has ever recorded. God has prospered our families, our lives. We don't talk about a television set. We talk about television *sets*. We don't talk about a car. We talk about cars; and if twenty years ago we could have been shown the house where most of us are living today, we would not have believed God could have done that for us.

Not only does God say you need to go on because of how He has prospered you, but He said, "You need to go on because of the way I've protected you." God says, "I have given you . . . cities which ye built not" (v. 13*b*). Cities were for protection. Cities were to protect the people from the attacks of the enemy. God has protected us. Just as He did for Job, God has built a hedge around our lives and our families. God has even protected our church family. Many things have happened over the last several years that could have absolutely destroyed our church and torn our church into pieces and forever ruined the church's witness, but God's hand stayed upon us. God's leadership was still here because God was protecting the fellowship known as San Jacinto Baptist Church.

Think about that time in your family when an illness struck your child, or think about that time when illness came to you, and God's hand of protection was there. God said, "I'm not finished with you yet." God has protected. His angels have camped about our homes at night, and God has protected us from the enemy and that which would hurt, and so God says, "Based on the way I've prospered you and protected you, how can you be hesitant to go on and be all I want you to be?"

Not only is His demonstration of care evident in the way He has prospered us and protected us, but also in the way He has provided for us. He said, ". . . of the vineyards and olive-yards which ye planted not do you eat" (v. 13c). Vineyards, throughout the Old Testament, referred to the Holy Spirit. The oil of the olives related to the oil of the Holy Spirit. What is He talking about? The miraculous provision of God for our lives. God has provided every single need that we have. Is there actually a need in your life that God has not met, that God has not provided for? We can rejoice with Paul that our God has supplied all our need, according to his riches in glory by Christ Jesus (see Phil. 4:19), and not one good word of His promise has ever failed. God has taken care of us. So God says to us, "Look at the way I've provided for you. Look at the way I've protected you. Look at the way I've prospered you."

On the local level, I think about how the Lord has provided for our church, the needs of the staff, the needs we have daily, the needs of ministry. God has provided for every need we have and, most of all, He has provided for our greatest need, the presence of His Holy Spirit every time we come together that makes our fellowship unique and different. It's the presence of the Holy Spirit of God when we come together. When people walk through the doors, they can feel, sense, and know there is a difference about it. The awe, the reverence, and the joy there are due to the presence of God's Holy Spirit. Pastors have come and gone, and yet that presence of God is continuing to be there. We praise God for that! God has provided for us; his oil is never going to fail. God's river of blessing is never going to run out. So God asks, "Based on my demonstration of care, why should you hesitate to make a commitment to go on?"

Second, not only does God give us a demonstration of

care, but God's challenge to us is also based on His demand for commitment. "Now, therefore, fear the Lord, and serve him in sincerity and in truth" (v. 14*a*). Because God has cared for you, prospered you, provided for you, and protected you, here's the challenge: "Fear the Lord and serve him in sincerity and in truth: and put away the gods which your fathers served on the other side of the flood, and in Egypt; and serve ye the Lord" (v. 14).

Look at this threefold command. First, it is *a command to worship*. "Fear the Lord." That is the number-one thing we must do if we are to reach a new commitment to be all God wants us to be. If we are to possess our possessions; if we are to claim all the promises of God; if we are to rise above the average, the mediocre, the carnal, the fleshly; if we are to be all God envisions us to be, we must learn to worship the Lord. That worship of the Lord, putting our eyes on Jesus Christ, makes us march to the beat of a different drummer. We must learn how to praise the Lord, magnify the Lord, love the Lord, express our hearts to the Lord, worship the Lord, and just sit at the feet of the Lord Jesus Christ and worship Him when we come together in our fellowship. That is the meaning of "Fear the Lord"—God's demand for worship. God wants us to worship Him. The Bible commands that we are to love Him with all our heart, with all our soul, with all our mind, and with all our strength. We will never be what God wants us to be until we reach the place where we can love Him with all of our being, all of our heart, all of our mind, all of our soul, and all of our strength.

I can imagine what God thinks about the average worship service in churches across this land. How it must break His heart to see people sleeping in churches. How it must break

His heart to see people sleeping while His Son is being preached and while His Son is being worshiped, or to see people with their minds on other matters. The difference in churches is commitment, and God demands a commitment of worship. We cannot begin to do what God wants until we have learned to sit at His feet, until we have learned to love Him and worship Him with all of our hearts.

Not only does this demand for commitment involve worship but, second, it involves a demand to work. He says, "Now therefore fear the Lord, and serve him in sincerity and in truth" (v. 14a). We have been learning that we are the body of Christ. As the body of Christ, we are to serve the Head. The Head tells the hands and the feet what to do. My hands are to serve my head. My feet are to serve my head. My head directs my entire body. Our Head is Jesus Christ, and the Bible teaches that there is a demand for work. We are to serve Him. We are living in a service-oriented society where people are used to going downtown and used to being served. They go to the shopping centers. It's difficult for twentieth-century Christians, living in America, to realize that the concept of the New Testament church is not being served, but serving others. That's what we're here to do—to serve Jesus. We are here to serve one another, and we are here to serve a lost and dying world. Here is a demand to work. It requires work to build a great church.

Why do you think it is, out of 36,000 Southern Baptist churches, so few are really great in terms of making an impact on their communities for God? Why do you think there are so few 3,000-seat worship centers across this land? I can tell you why. It is because it takes W-O-R-K. It takes being in church for visitation, being there Sunday night for services, teaching that Sunday School class, being that outreach leader, working on that bus route. When we reach the point where we are just interested in the kind of church that is going to serve us, work for us, and meet our needs, then we have left the realm of the blessing of God upon us, because God blesses work. God blesses service.

Jesus was a worker. Jesus said, "My Father has sent me, I have come to do the work of my Father." He said, "The night is coming when no man can work" (John 9:4, Author's words). Jesus knew what it was to sweat and to work. Many churches today have only one service—on Sunday morning. They have no Sunday night service or Wednesday night service. Everything is for the convenience of people. Everything is to meet the whims of people, and I believe we are growing a Christianity in many cases that is fat and lazy, and that God cannot bless. No wonder the world is dying and going to hell. Nobody much wants to work anymore. Nobody much wants to serve anymore. To enlist Sunday School teachers, you have to beg people because they are going to be "inconvenienced." They are going to have to spend some time in preparation. Some things are going to be required of them. Try to line up bus workers, and you can't do it because no one wants to visit every Saturday. Why is that? We've lost the vision for work, and this is a demand for work.

Not only is it a demand for work, it is *a demand for witness*. It says that we are to "put away the gods which your fathers served on the other side of the flood, and in Egypt; and serve ye the Lord." It's talking about the purity of our lives. I'm convinced with all of my heart that we need a revival of holiness and purity, a cleansing of the people of God. If what you call your salvation experience did not cause you to put away the gods of this world and serve God out of a pure heart, than it wasn't a real salvation experience. The Bible says, "If any man be in Christ, he is a new creature [creation]" (2 Cor. 5:17).

God says, "I want you to go on. Don't stay where you are. Don't be satisfied with what I have already given you. Don't be satisfied with the land you've conquered—there's more to conquer. Go on and be everything that I want you to be."

Third, not only is there a demonstration of care and a demand for commitment, but He mentions here a *decision of certainty*. "If it seem evil unto you to serve the Lord, choose you this day whom ye will serve; whether the gods which your fathers served that were on the other side of the flood, or the gods of the Amorites, in whose land ye dwell: but as for me and my house, we will serve the Lord" (v. 15).

If we are going to be all God wants us to be, there needs to be a decision of certainty. If you've "plateaued" where you are, and you can feel yourself sliding backward in the Christian life, all that is going to turn you around is a decision of certainty. This is a message to people who are already the people of God, people who have fought many battles and won those battles, people who have already conquered much ground. Here He's not talking to a lost world. He's saying to the people of God, "I'm calling you to a new commitment. I'm calling you to a new decision," and He said, "Here's the decision."

First, you have three choices. (1) You can serve the gods which your fathers served on the other side of the river, and I see in that, tradition. You can serve tradition. That's where many churches are today. If you didn't sing the Doxology in some churches, they'd think the world had come to an end. In some churches they think if you let out one minute past twelve o'clock, you have violated biblical principles. There are many people who have Baptist tradition mixed up with Bible doctrine. We must not be more loyal to the name Baptist than we are to the Word of God. I'm a Baptist, but if Southern Baptists ever depart from this Book, I'm going to be something else. I'm going to stay with the Book of books. I'm going to stick with the Word of God.

I cannot go along with those who preach and teach that the Old Testament is legend, myth, and mere folklore, and not literal history. I cannot walk with those who contend that the first eleven chapters of Genesis are not the literal Word of God. The written Word of God is inerrant, and I contend that what we believe about the Word of God, the Bible, is extremely important. Yet there are some people who declare, "I'm a Baptist (or Methodist or Presbyterian or Lutheran, whatever) forever, no mater what." I cannot buy into that. You talk about diversity. Baptists are as diverse in their belief as the East is from the West. Some of us are closer to the Assemblies of God and some of the Bible churches than we are to some of our Baptist brethren. We can't serve the gods of tradition and go on for God; we can't serve the gods our fathers served, doing things the way our fathers did because our fathers did it. We can become soft and comfortable with that kind of doctrine and die on the vine.

He says, "Here's one of your choices—tradition. You can simply serve the gods your fathers served." Second, He said, "Or you can serve the gods of this world. You can serve the gods of the Amorites, in whose land you dwell." Many Christians are doing that. They are serving the gods of the world.

They are serving the god of success, the god of money, the god of power, and the god of pride. They have been caught up in the things of this world, and they are serving the gods of the Amorites.

What happened to the people of God? The people of God moved into the land and rather than being witnesses for God and winning those people, those people began to influence the people of God. The people of God became like the people of the world instead of the other way around. They began to serve the gods of the Amorites, in whose land they dwelled.

We can do that. To a great extent in most churches, people are going through the motions of religion and going through the rituals of religion, but such doesn't change their lives. There's no power of God. There's no breath of the Holy Spirit of God, no life-changing power, no witness, no compelling drive to get out and reach people for Jesus Christ. We can do likewise. That is one of the choices we have. Serve the gods of this world six days a week, and come to church on Sunday. That's easy to do. It would be far easier, as a preacher, to be that kind of preacher and to preach in that kind of church and live in that kind of ivory tower. If that's the choice we make, then we are never going to conquer the land and never going to possess what God wants us to have.

Your third choice is this. He said, ". . . [or] serve ye the Lord." He said, "If it seems evil unto you to serve the Lord, choose you this day whom ye will serve." That's our choice. You can serve the Lord. That's the demand of commitment. It's a decision of certainty.

There are two or three things about this decision. First, it's *personal*. The choice you have to make is personal in your life. Nobody can choose to go on for God for you, but you.

You're the only one who can make that choice and that commitment. Whatever the church decides as a body, it's still going to be up to individuals.

One of the problems we have is that sometimes the church makes a decision, and then people don't make that commitment in their own personal lives. It's a personal choice. Joshua said, "But as for me, I'm going to serve the Lord. I'm going to make that commitment. I'm going to go on and be all God wants me to be." Many folks haven't even made a commitment to tithe, much less to give of themselves, or to give over and above the tithe, and give of their hearts to serve God with all that they are. It's a personal commitment to be all God wants you to be.

Daniel Webster was going to be a lawyer. Of course, he became a famous lawyer and a noted legislator. He was told when he was a young man not to go into the practice of law because that field was already overrun by lawyers. He answered, "I know it, but there's plenty of room at the top."

When it comes to the commitment of God's people, there's plenty of room at the top. I believe that God is challenging us, individually, to go on and be all He wants us to be. Are we willing to pay the price to rise above the average, to rise above the mediocre? If we would pay the price for the power of God, we could win our city to Christ in less than a year. If we would be willing to make the commitment it takes, there's no limit to what God could do in us and through us. It's yet to be seen what the Lord could do through a totally committed person and through a totally committed church.

Second, it has to be *positive*. Joshua said, "As for me and my house, we will serve the Lord." He was saying, "I don't care what anybody else does. If everybody else turns back, if everybody else is satisfied, if everybody else sits down, if everybody else says, 'I'm not going to do it,' if everybody else says that it can't be done, if everybody else says, 'We've done enough,' if everybody else says, 'I'm not going to do it,'" Joshua says he's going to do it." He made a positive decision and a positive commitment. Not only was it personal and positive but it was *public*.

Everyone was influenced by his decision. His family was influenced. All of Israel was influenced. People are influenced by our lives, either for God or for Satan, good or bad. We need to challenge one another and motivate one another. We need to encourage one another. We need to build a fire under one another. We need to stir up one another in a positive kind of way. What I do affects you. If I'm satisfied with the average, if I'm satisfied with the mediocre, if I'm satisfied just to get by, if I'm satisfied with where we are now, you are going to be satisfied, and the same is true in the leadership position you hold. God wants to do more, but we will have to challenge one another and be willing to make that commitment.

Last of all, it was *prompt*. He said, "Choose you this day whom ye will serve." There's always an urgency about God. It can never wait until tomorrow, until next week, or next year. We must invite the lost, "Come to Christ today. Jesus may come soon." We urge the lost, "Come to Christ today, the Holy Spirit may not call you again." There is an urgency about people being saved, about the work of God, about your Christian life. If you don't become what God wants you to be today, then you may never become what God wants you to be tomorrow. If you don't make the right decision and the right commitment today, then you may never be able to make the right decision or the right commitment tomorrow.

There's a drastic urgency. It's time to fall on our faces before God. It's now or never. The choice is for us to go on and be all God wants us to be, not to settle for less, not to settle for second best, but to become all the Lord wants us to be.

10

It's Amazing What Praising Can Do!

And the multitude rose up together against them: and the magistrates rent off their clothes, and commanded to beat them.

And when they had laid many stripes upon them, they cast them into the prison, charging the jailer to keep them safely:

Who, having received such a charge, thrust them into the inner prison, and made their feet fast in the stocks.

And at midnight Paul and Silas prayed, and sang praises unto God: and the prisoners heard them.

And suddenly there was a great earthquake, so that the foundations of the prison were shaken: and immediately all the doors were opened, and every one's bands were loosed.

And the keeper of the prison awaking out of his sleep, and seeing the prison doors open, he drew out his sword, and would have killed himself, supposing that the prisoners had been fled.

But Paul cried with a loud voice, saying, Do thyself no harm: for we are all here.

Then he called for a light, and sprang in, and came trembling, and fell down before Paul and Silas,

And brought them out, and said, Sirs, what must I do to be saved?

And they said, Believe on the Lord Jesus Christ, and thou shalt be saved, and thy house.

And he took them the same hour of the night, and washed their stripes; and was baptized, he and all his, straightway.

And when he had brought them into his house, he set meat before them, and rejoiced, believing in God with all his house.

Acts 16:22-34

In 1 Thessalonians 5:18 Paul wrote, "In every thing give thanks: for this is the will of God in Christ Jesus concerning you." Paul practiced what he preached. In the sixteenth chapter of the Book of Acts, we are going to view a time when Paul and his fellow laborer, Silas, praised God at midnight.

It's easy to praise God when it's light and you can see, when life is going well and the bank account is solvent, when there is no ill health and no difficulty, but can you praise God at midnight? This is what happened in the life of Paul.

These two men of God, Paul and Silas, had been preaching the Word of God. They had been walking down the center of God's will for their lives, and where did it land them? In jail (vs. 22-24). They were put in the innermost prison where the light could not shine, and the stench was unbearable. They were put into stocks where their limbs were stretched out of their sockets, and they were there in the darkness with rats running across their feet, and the Bible tells us their reaction in verses 25 through 31.

Praise at midnight will have many beneficial results. Maybe you are in a situation where you cannot seem to change the circumstances. It may be an economic reverse, a problem in your marriage, an illness in your family. It may be midnight in your life for many reasons, and discouragement, doubt, and depression have set in. You have struggled, cried, prayed, sought counsel, read the Bible, and done everything you know to do, and nothing has helped. But let me encourage you at the midnight hour to praise God! When Paul and Silas prayed and sang praises to God at midnight, God began to move tremendously in their lives.

You must understand that in the Bible we are not only commanded to pray, but we are commanded to praise the Lord in all things. Many think it is very foolish for me to tell you to praise God for the bad things, as well as the good things, but the Bible says, "In every thing give thanks." There is a reason why God wants us to praise Him at the midnight hour when we cannot see our way, when we feel we are doing the best we can. We're serving God, and suddenly the bottom of life drops out, and we don't know where to turn or what we are going to do. At midnight you can praise the Lord. Praising God at midnight can work wonders in your life.

Praising God at midnight will recognize the sovereignty of God. When you praise God in a difficult time, you are recognizing that God is in charge, that He is in control. Sometimes we're tempted to think that when we have problems, we must be out of the will of God. We're tempted to think that difficulties say to us that God is not pleased, that God is not blessing. I know Paul and Silas were directly in the center of God's will for their lives, and yet they found that the pathway of obedience is also the pathway of suffering. It's like that many times in our lives. When we can praise God at the midnight hour, we are recognizing that nothing can happen to us outside the permissive will of God for our lives, and nothing can happen to us that God cannot take, turn around, and use for our good and for His glory.

That is exactly what happened when Jesus went to the cross. That was the greatest injustice ever done and the darkest hour mankind has ever seen, and yet today we look at the Cross and to the glorious resurrection and realize that at the midnight hour, when Jesus cried on the cross, God was doing a marvelous work. When you praise God in the darkness, you are recognizing the sovereignty of God. You are acknowledging that even though things are difficult and times are hard, nothing can happen to you that God cannot turn around and use for your good and His glory. God is so committed to you, so caring for you, so loving of you, and so aware of you, that He is going to work in spite of all the difficulties you face.

We sing a chorus that goes, "Our God Reigns." He does! When we praise God, that is what we are acknowledging. The psalmist said, "I will bless the Lord at all times: his praise shall continually be in my mouth" (Ps. 34:1).

Paul and Silas were in the darkness during that difficult time, with every nerve in their bodies a path upon which the feet of pain would run. Their backs were bloody, they were in those stocks, they were in the darkness, and Paul may have asked, "Well, Silas, what are we going to do in this situation?" Silas may well have suggested, "Paul, I don't know what you are going to do, but I'm going to praise the Lord." They began to praise God at midnight because they recognized that God was in charge, God was in control of the situation, and they could trust Him.

Not only will praise *recognize sovereignty,* praise will *resist Satan.* You see, the devil had come against these two men, and he had decided he didn't like what God was doing to and through them, and he was going to stop the revival. They were thrown into jail. The devil thought he was eliminating the revival. He wasn't doing that—he just changed its location. He got it off the street and into the jailhouse where everyone was lost and needed to hear the gospel.

Many times when the devil comes against us, if we will, in the midst of that situation, praise the Lord, God will use it against the devil and turn the situation around. Then what the devil meant for ill and evil, God will use for our good. The devil can't stay very long around a Christian who is praising the Lord. The devil can't abide a service where people are praising the Lord. The demons of hell hate to hear the name of Jesus lifted up, and they despise hearing Jesus praised.

The devil is allergic to praise. That's why it is doubly important that we learn to praise God at the midnight hour because Satan is going to come against us. Exactly at the time when we think our problems are gone and we have everything under control, things are going to come loose and are going to get completely out of hand. We need to understand that we have an enemy. We don't "wrestle against flesh and blood, but against principalities, against powers, against the rulers of the darkness of this world, against spiritual wickedness in high places" (Eph. 6:12). The only way to defeat this enemy is through praise. Have you tried praise today? In the circumstance you have no control over, with that unyielding wall that is a blockade in your life, in that difficulty going on right now, have you tried praising the Lord? At midnight, Paul and Silas sang praises unto God.

Not only will praise recognize God's sovereignty and resist Satan, but praise will *release the Spirit*. The Bible teaches that, as they began to praise God, He began to move because, not only did Satan hear their praise, but God heard their praise as well. The Lord must have been watching from heaven. When He saw those two men begin to praise Him in spite of the pain and suffering they were in, I think He must have said, "Angels, come over here. Angels, look down there. Angels, do you see what my servants are doing? They've been persecuted and punished. They're in tremendous pain and are confined in darkness, but, angels, do you hear what they are doing? Angels, isn't that the sweetest song you've ever heard? They're praising Me." Then I think God must have said, "Earthquake Angel, go down there and shake that prison, I'm going to show those people a thing or two." You see, God begins to work when we begin to praise.

From the Bible, we see that God always fought for His people, and God always won for His people. He won the day when His people started to praise Him.

It happened in the lives of Jehosaphat, Jonah, and David. When the people of God begin to praise Him, He begins to work. God begins to shake things.

Verse 25 ". . . and the prisoners heard them." The prisoners had never heard anything like that before. The word for *hear*, used in this case, is not the ordinary Greek word for *hear*. It means to hear attentively, to hear with the heart. When they began to sing about the greatness and power of God, the blood of Jesus Christ and the power in the name of Christ, God began to convict the hearts of those prisoners. They heard about how Jesus could save and deliver. Those prisoners had never heard anything like it. Maybe they'd heard "Folsom Prison Blues" but never the "Hallelujah Chorus." A little humor there! I mean this was the first sacred concert in all of Europe. It was like a Hale and Wilder duet—only it was Paul and Silas. The text states in verse 26, ". . . so that the foundations of the prison were shaken." God began to shake that place because His men praised Him at midnight.

No matter how bad things become around the church or how difficult our problems or how big the challenge before us or what happens in our homes, it may be the midnight hour, but when we begin to praise God, God begins to move, releasing His Spirit, and the Spirit of God begins to shake things. The foundations of hell would be shaken more if God's people would not complain and criticize or doubt and fear in the midnight hour. Learn to praise God. When you do God will begin to shake the foundations of hell, the prison doors of sin will open, and those who are shackled and chained by sin will be set free—if the people of God would ever learn to praise the Lord.

One of the main activities in heaven is going to be praise? We are going to spend all of eternity praising God. Praise God, I want to get in practice down here, don't you? I don't want God to have to put me in praise school when I reach heaven and say, "You never learned how to praise Me." We must learn how to praise God, and then we need to praise Him at midnight.

Praise releases the power of the Spirit. The foundations of the prison were shaken. Praise will do something else—it will *redeem the sinner*. The text says that the jailer also heard what was going on. Notice how praise redeemed this man's life. We know he was changed by the power of God because the man had seen the worst of people. Those who work around jails and are on the police force are exposed to life at its rawest. This man had become hardened in his heart. He could put those men in stocks and torture them and not bat an eyelash. He was tough, not the kind of man who came to Sunday School and loved God.

This was not the kind of man you could reach through ordinary methods. It was going to take a crisis in his case. There are so many people God wants to reach, but it requires a trauma for God to reach them. They have so hardened their hearts against God that their baby would have to be dying before they would wake up or their wife would have to leave them or their business would have to collapse. God would have to send a crisis in their life. If God has to send a crisis, He certainly knows how to do it.

An earthquake hit the jail, all the prison's doors were opened, and he thought the prisoners had escaped. He had been warned that if any of his prisoners escaped, his life would be taken in their place; so he had pulled out his sword, thinking that was the end. He was about to commit hari kari, about to fall on his sword, because he thought there was no hope. It was a tremendous crisis in his life.

About that time, Paul stayed his hand with "Do thyself no harm: for we are all here" (v. 28). I believe none of them escaped because they all got saved! Their hearts had been changed, and they weren't going to escape. Paul explained "We're all here. [We're just sitting here obediently in these cells under the civil authority. You don't have to kill yourself]."

Then the jailer called for a light. Praise and the supernatural power of God had brought him under conviction until the Bible says that he came before Paul and Silas, trembling. He was shaking so badly that someone else had to hold the light. He wanted to see for himself that every prisoner was in his place. When he saw that none of those men had escaped, he fell down before Paul and Silas and implored, "What must I do to be saved?" (v. 30).

Praise brought conviction in the jailer's life when he heard Paul and Silas praising God. When the power of God was released, through praise, to work in that prison and in that man's life, he cried out, "What must I do to be saved?"

If we'll learn to praise God at the midnight hour, if we'll continually bless the Lord at all times, if God's praise would continually be in our mouths, we'd have people coming, falling on their knees, and begging, "Tell us how to be saved. Tell us about Jesus." Paul answered the jailer, "Believe on the Lord Jesus Christ and thou shalt be saved."

The word *believe* in verse 31 does not just mean an intellectual assent, but it is an action word. *Believe* in the Bible is a commitment word. Paul was telling him to commit his life to, rely upon, and trust Jesus. Salvation is not merely having your name on a church roll. Salvation is a commitment of your life.

Notice not only the commitment of his life but the change in the jailer's life. He took Paul and Silas, whom he had thrown into prison and whom he had beaten on their backs, washed their stripes, put medicine on their wounds, fixed them a meal, and sat them down at his own table in his own house. Here was a man who had been totally changed by the power of God, and God had moved potently in this man's life. A change comes about when Jesus is invited in. Notice the contentment in his life. The Bible points out that he was rejoicing with all his household in the Lord.

I've seen many drab church members, but I'm not sure I've ever really seen drab Christians. The jailer had been saved, and he was rejoicing. He came in the right way. He came in under praise, and now he was praising God. There is a contentment that could enter your life. In spite of the darkness of the midnight hour when your heart is breaking, when it is dark, and you can't see any purpose or reason for the circumstances of your life, you could have rejoicing in your heart through the power of Jesus Christ if only you will commit your life to Him.

At midnight, Paul and Silas sang praises unto God. And you can, too!

About the Author

Dr. Stan Coffey is senior pastor of the San Jacinto Baptist Church, Amarillo, Texas, where he has served twice—first from October 1975 to September 1979 and second from June 1984 until present. The church recently completed a 3,000-seat worship center. He has served as president of the SBC Pastors' Conference (1987-1988).

A native of Oklahoma, Coffey was reared "in the nurture and admonition of the Lord" on a farm near Sweetwater. At the age of six he was saved in a small Southern Baptist church nearby.

He married the former Glenda Fincher of Elk City, Oklahoma, in 1962. She is the daughter of a Baptist minister. Stan and Glenda have two children, Scott and Natalie.

Coffey is a graduate of Sweetwater High School, Wayland Baptist University (B.A.), and Southwestern Baptist Theological Seminary (M.R.E.). The California Graduate School of Theology honored him with the D.D.

His wife, Glenda, attended Amarillo College, Amarillo, Texas, and the University of New Mexico, Albuquerque. She has actively served in every phase of church life, particularly with young adults. She led the Young Adult Sunday School Division at San Jacinto from an attendance of twenty to more than 100. At First, Albuquerque, she directed the Young Adult Division to grow from forty to 140. During college and seminary days, Glenda was known as a capable business woman, working in banking and financial institutions in almost every capacity from bookkeeping to commercial loans. She is currently directing the Women's Bible Study at San Jacinto and is involved in organizing women's rallies and luncheons.

Dr. Coffey's pastorates during college and seminary days were County Line Baptist Church, Morton; Hurlwood, Lubbock; First, Josephine; and Trinity, Texarkana, all in Texas.

The first time he pastored at San Jacinto there was a total of 3,575 additions in four years, 2,187 by baptism, and a total of 3,000 professions of faith. Sunday School attendance grew from an average of 400 to more than 1,500. The church led the Texas Baptist Convention in 1979 with 1,263 baptisms.

He then served First Baptist Church of Albuquerque, New Mexico, for almost five years. In what is commonly considered a "pioneer" area for Southern Baptist work, there were more than 3,200 additions to the church. More than 2,200 were by baptism, with a total of 2,500 professions of faith. The church broke all New Mexico evangelistic records and led the state in baptisms for five years. Consistent leaders in evangelism, Dr. Coffey's churches have baptized an average of 700 persons per year for the past five years.

In addition to being president of the Southern Baptist Pastors' Conference, Coffey has been vice-president of the Conference. He was chairman of the Order of Business Committee of the Convention (1986-1987) and has been a member of the SBC Committee on Committees (1981-1982). He has been pastor-advisor to the Southern Baptist Convention Evangelists Conference and also to the Conference of Texas Baptist Evangelists.

Coffey has preached 120 revival meetings in several states and has been on the program of numerous state evangelistic conferences. When he takes time off he fishes, hunts, and gardens.

Other Books to Help You
Build the Greatest Churches Since Pentecost

Mastering Your Emotions by **Adrian P. Rogers**

Dr. Rogers helps the reader to understand his emotions and deal with them constructively, feelings like doubt, insecurity, fear, bitterness, bewilderment, frustration, loneliness, and others. He writes with sound principles from Christian psychology and God's written Word, the Bible.

Here is a treasure of personal assistance which will aid the reader in having a realistic assessment of his emotions and then working through them to a happier, healthier outlook. The book is filled with resource material for counseling, preaching, and teaching.

Confronting Casual Christianity by **Charles F. Stanley**

Dr. Stanley issues a call to total commitment. In this book he challenges Christians to meet head-on the complacency of their individual lives and the collective lives of their churches. He writes: "The severest sin of Christians is a numbing lack of concern, an anesthetized attitude of 'I don't care. I'm in the fold. Why should I concern myself?'"

Stanley writes that the Lordship of Christ is central, calling for *commitment* and *obedience*. The Bible-based principles of this book will open your eyes that you may see, free your minds that you may think on Him, loosen your tongues to sing His praises and witness for Him, activate your feet to "go" for Him, and energize your entire being to confront casual Christianity.

God's Way to Health, Wealth, and Wisdom
by Adrian P. Rogers

Dr. Rogers steers his readers onto the true path to health, wealth, and wisdom. From the word go, he makes it plain that health, wealth, and wisdom are not found in "pop" psychology, "hocus pocus," or a misapplication of the Bible's truth—but in an acceptance of the clear teachings of God's Word, not a distorted view that contends health, wealth, and wisdom are one's possession through the snap of a finger.

Some of his chapters are: How Not to Raise a Fool, Finding God's Way in a Dark Day, The Playboy's Pay Day, God's Grace in the Work Place, The Friendship Factor, God's Answer to Anger, and God's Miracle Medicine.

Nothing But the Blood by Bailey E. Smith

Evangelist Bailey E. Smith's theme in *Nothing But the Blood* is Christ crucified, buried, resurrected, ascended, and coming again. Here is a choice collection of Dr. Smith's preaching on the sacrificial death of the Lord Jesus Christ on the Cross.

Dr. Smith's convincing messages are: The Motivating Power of the Cross, Offended by the Opportunity to Live, The Problems of Pilate, The Words Jesus Spoke from the Cross (Parts I and II), The Secret of Ultimate Living, What a Difference Easter Makes, The Man Who Wore the First Jesus Shirt, The Cross and Compassion, The Convincing Power of the Cross, Nothing But the Blood, and Bearing the Cross.

The Unveiling by James T. Draper, Jr.

Dr. James T. Draper, Jr., has written a thorough treatment of The Revelation, the Apocalypse, from the dispensational premillennial view. He believes that the Lord Jesus is coming back before the Tribulation period and that believers will be caught up with Him in the Rapture. After the Tribulation period, then Christ will come to earth with all the believers of the ages to rule in His millennial kingdom.

Several of his chapters are: The Heavenly Throne, Worthy Is the Lamb, The Great Tribulation, The World's Greatest Revival, The Trumpet Judgments, The Angel and the Scroll, The Two Witnesses, The Antichrist, The Seven Bowls of Wrath, Babylon the Great, The Millennial Reign, The Great White Throne, and more.